Integrating New Approaches

The Teaching of French in Higher Education

Edited by James A. Coleman
and Annie Rouxeville

Published by the Association for French Language Studies in association with the Centre for Information on Language Teaching and Research, 20 Bedfordbury, London WC2N 4LB.
Printed in Great Britain by Middlesex University Printing Unit.

First published 1993.

ISBN 1 874016 09 7

In Memory of Adrian Battye

Contents

Introduction

Integrating New Approaches: the Teaching of French in Higher Education appears at a time of virtually unprecedented change within the profession, with pressures coming simultaneously from a number of directions:

- the expansion of the university sector to absorb the former polytechnics;

- the rapid advances in technology which in less than twenty years have turned computers and satellite television from the exotic to the banal, and have seen multimedia grow from a futuristic dream to an affordable reality;

- the changes in the funding of both teaching and research which are characterised by reduction, redistribution and uncertainty;

- the very considerable expansion in numbers of language undergraduates, which may now cease following the change in government policy;

- the accelerating europeanisation of courses through ERASMUS and LINGUA;

- the move from single degrees to a unit/credit system and from terms to semesters in over 80% of higher education institutions;

- the change in focus from a largely staff-centred to a largely student-centred ethos;

- increased reliance, for both methodological and economic reasons, on self-access learning;

- the new approach to research degrees, with emphasis on completion rates and time taken;

- the Languages For All and Institution Wide Language Programmes which have meant that the area of most rapid expansion in French and other language studies is in language training for specialists in other disciplines - some 30,000 of them in 1991-92[1];

- developments in applied linguistics, in areas such as second language acquisition and language testing, which throw ever more light on the shortcomings of some current practice;

- the restructuring of administration and management in many institutions;

- the increased reliance on part-time teachers, averaging 19% of staff nationally, but over 50% in many places[2].

The reader can no doubt add more examples of changes which have radically altered the professional life of the language specialist in British higher education.

In such a context, we felt that a book devoted to the theoretical basis for new approaches, and to some of the practical issues they raise, would be most timely. Our original notion was that the methodological innovations of the past few years were now reasonably well assimilated, but that the practical *integration* of research findings, and of such tools as authentic written and spoken texts, computer-assisted language learning, and tailor-made open access facilities was still problematic on many French courses. This does indeed seem to be the case, and the present volume contains examples of good practice which may give guidance to those seeking to integrate new approaches without losing coherence, without disrupting existing courses and without undermining staff morale. The response to our invitation to contributors was, however, broader than we had anticipated, and contributions to the book do go beyond the French (or indeed Spanish or German) course itself to look at the climate of multiple change alluded to above.

The different papers, covering disparate areas, may well correspond to the experience of many readers: they provide an awareness both of the diversity of available approaches and of the potential of bringing them together for the benefit of the learner. The chapters are not all at the frontiers of research (basic, strategic, applied or otherwise), but they do all seek to help bring up to date readers who may have an incomplete acquaintance with an individual subject. One message which emerges clearly from the book is that, faced with the new challenges of the 1990s, there is a whole range of new approaches, tools and materials which is available to the teacher of modern languages in British colleges and universities.

* * *

Ignorance has undoubtedly been one reason for retaining, unquestioned, methods and materials from a previous age, when the desired outcomes of higher education were rarely defined except in the most general terms, when the science of linguistics was in its infancy, and when an approach based on the teaching of dead languages was deemed, intuitively, appropriate also for *langues vivantes*. It is clear, not least from some of the articles which were *not* accepted for the present collection, that ignorance - both of current theoretical knowledge and of current practice within the sector - remains a problem. It is, at the very least, understandable, if not actually forgivable, that university staff, from whom an increasing research output is expected in an often wholly different research domain, typically literature or area studies (to achieve promotion, it is alleged that language teachers have to publish twice as much!), might be unaware of the detail of some very recent developments in language learning research. But for such ignorance to be widespread must reflect ultimately on the professional competence, and professional credibility, of university language teachers as a whole. As one referee commented on a rejected paper, "I had almost forgotten why we need postgraduate training in language studies. Hélas, I have remembered."

What other trends can be discerned? In terms of staffing, the largest area of growth is in language teaching to students specialising in subjects other than languages - an issue of direct concern to Michèle Dickson and Margaret Parry, and alluded to in several other papers. Some colleagues who feel threatened by this development, which is, *avouons-le*, in part dictated by pragmatic, even basely materialist, considerations on the part of our students, would like to conclude from it that the language learning part of a French or German degree curriculum is the mechanistic acquisition of a "mere" skill, and that the real value of such a degree lies elsewhere, in the cognitive and personal, intellectual and spiritual development fostered by the "content" part of the syllabus, whether literary or otherwise. There are two answers to this essentially defensive posture.

On the one hand, where is the evidence that the more traditional degree programmes produced the well-rounded, sensitive, capable individuals they claimed? Is it a shared perception that, while naïveté and immaturity are inevitably reduced by the four years, including a year's residence abroad, that turn student teens into twenties, it is not conclusively demonstrated that an arts degree necessarily inculcates the skills of analysis and synthesis commonly claimed for it?

Imported definitions of quality as "fitness for purpose(s), where the purpose is determined by the customer for the service" have met with hostility in the universities[3], not least because the definition of our "customers" is so complex: they include present and potential students, parents, employers, the government, the local community and society in general, and the relationship is in any case not analogous to that of a supplier of cars or chewing gum. Additionally, there is confusion over exactly what customers want, and over what a traditional modern languages degree claims to offer.

David Nott is perhaps exceptional in defining in precise terms those competences which students of, say, French language and literature are expected to gain from their studies. Most definitions are vague, bordering on the lyrical. They tend to talk of traditional academic virtues without defining what they are: "literature is a repository of humane and moral values, a civilising influence"[4] with a "unique relationship to human experience"[5], offering "illumination to individuals and nations alike ... [and defining] ... the conditions of human creativity and the terms of humanity's wager with God, history, nature"[6].

Anyone who has taught literature knows the satisfaction of helping students to awaken to the aesthetic qualities of a text - perhaps for the first time. But few would deny that much student work in the field consists of a mechanical regurgitation or a reshaping of second-hand material.

Some claim literature teaches a sense of values, although given that the standard choice of texts in French studies runs from *Manon Lescaut* and *Les Liaisons Dangereuses* through *Madame Bovary*, *Les Fleurs du Mal* and *L'Assommoir* to *L'Immoraliste* and *A la Recherche du Temps perdu* - a cumulative portrait of social and sexual mores which would put in the shade even the behaviour of our present royal family as catalogued in the yellow press - the process is evidently one of inverse osmosis. If empirical evidence exists that modern language graduates are either more cultured or more moral than, say, biochemists or electrical engineers, that evidence should be more widely disseminated.

By another typical definition, students of French seek, as well as language skills, "the breadth of intellectual and moral vision, and the incisiveness, confidence and humanity which come with scholarly exploration of a great cultural heritage"[7]. This contrasts with a rather less traditional view, which suggests[8]: "Most undergraduates studying languages today expect to master both academic and professional or technical skills - receptive, productive, analytical and social - which will help to prepare them for their potential career. Typically these skills would include:

- Intellectual training in analysis, logical argument and independent thinking.

- An awareness of contemporary issues and ideas.

- The ability to perform both academic and real life tasks in situations, ranging from contact with administration and the employment context to social interaction with friends or colleagues."

The objectives of many modern language degrees, then, remain vague. Moreover, the present system of degree classes, with their secrecy and intuitive criteria, further helps obscure what it is a language graduate might be expected to know or do: profiling will be a welcome replacement here. Yet there *is* evidence of what both students and employers are seeking from university studies, and it is often not what traditional humanities graduates have to offer. It is increasingly manifest - not least from the chapters of this book and in its predecessor, *French and the Enterprise Path: developing transferable and professional skills*, as well as elsewhere[9] - that the activities and exercises now used to expand language competence are also precisely those activities which stretch the social, cognitive and intellectual abilities of our students and prepare them for adult life. Geoffrey Hare and Phil Powrie identified "transferable social skills - group work, setting and meeting objectives, making presentations, preparing reports, numeracy, etc." and "excellent communication skills (both oral and written), ability to work effectively in a team, quickness to take sound initiatives, adeptness at managing themselves, their workload, and others, enthusiasm, and high self-motivation and an ability to motivate and inspire others" as qualities seen as desirable by potential employers, and built them in as objectives to their business studies option at Newcastle[10]. At Salford, too, explicit objectives are built into French and other degree courses:

"All students shall have developed all or most of the following skills/competencies:

a)   to negotiate, as they arrange details of project work with staff

b)   to plan, as they formulate their group plans for their project work

c)   to manage time effectively, as they deliver agreed work on time

d)   to work effectively towards a common goal in an organised and effective manner

e)   to provide and respond to leadership and select their own leaders for different tasks

f)   to learn how to learn more effectively

g)   to make a point and argue a case

h)   to write succinct reports for a variety of readers

i)   to give presentations either singly or in groups, of the results of their work

j)   to prepare job descriptions, apply for jobs and conduct interview panels to interview their peers and vice versa

k)   to prepare for, run and minute meetings effectively

l)   to be familiar with computers, using word-processors, spread sheets and data bases for written work and financial manipulations

m)   to analyse open-ended problems and derive cost-effective solutions

n)   to develop a greater understanding of employment and industry, including the need to be effective in a European context

o)   to learn specific management topics such as marketing and business finance where appropriate, where possible from employers."[11]

Additionally, no contemporary definition of the linguistic competence we expect from our graduates would exclude the socio-cultural domain, which is peripheral and subordinate to sociolinguistic competence for theorists such as

Munby, Canale and Swain, Hymes and Bachmann, but which motivates the increasing alliance between languages and area studies. The theme of learning a foreign culture while also studying its language is treated in an innovative way by Ana Barro and Hanns Grimm - though they extend the notion beyond what is current practice in most departments today - and forms a key factor in the argumentation of Dickson, Inkster and Nott. "Language learning", then, is more than just a skill, more than just a knowledge base, but *demonstrably* incorporates other competences.

We should perhaps make clear that we do not believe a traditional humanities degree cannot develop a student's intellectual, social and cognitive faculties, just that in today's climate there is a need to state explicitly what the course objectives are and how staff, students and "customers" of all kinds can measure the achievement of those objectives.

* * *

If language teaching is sometimes less effective than it might be - and we contend this is still too often the case - it is partly due to the low status accorded to this area of professional activity, despite the lip-service paid (but for how much longer?) to the notion of the teacher-researcher. Language-teaching is demoted to a non-specialist activity which anyone can - indeed, everyone must - perform, like invigilating first-year exams or putting more paper in the photocopier. Training in the processes involved in language learning remains the exception. Attitude, which plays such a crucial role in the degree of success of the language acquisition process, unsurprisingly determines also the degree of professional conscientiousness displayed by individual members of staff in their language teaching.

There is apparently little scientific data available on whether in fact higher education language teachers are generally putting up-to-date theory into practice, or whether, despite a putative lack of theoretical knowledge, their practice is nonetheless effective. Both are areas for urgent research[12], in which AFLS will shortly be involved. There is, however, data collected in 1986 from a representative sample of 586 students for the Nuffield Modern Languages Inquiry. Dr Paul Meara has analysed some of the data in three so far unpublished reports, and they show extensive traditionalism in language departments. Despite the widespread criticism of the grammar-translation method of language teaching in the literature, most students in 1986 spent about 20% of their weekly study time on translation, with three quarters spending at least two hours a week on each of L1>L2 and L2>L1 translation - an outstanding example of unawareness of the research literature that in most domains would amount to professional suicide, but which a number of factors, including research specialisms, lack of staff training and development, and perhaps the old-boy network of external examiners has sustained to this day: a study of final language exams by George Evans in February 1993 shows the prose and *version* alive and kicking in the traditional universities, despite more innovative assessments in many. Of thirty respondents, all but one include a prose in the final assessment, and in half of them students' written skills are evaluated *only* by means of a prose and essay.

The Nuffield students of 1986 rejected what are, arguably, the linguistic objectives of traditional courses. "To discuss the arts in a formal social setting" mattered to only 10% of students, and the ability to function as a translator or interpreter (assuming they could!) to only 20%. The survey thus "suggests that the consensus that exists among language teachers about the reasons for learning and teaching languages may not in fact be shared by those that they teach".

Only one third of the respondents (77% of whom were from traditional universities, and only 23% from what were then public sector institutions) felt literary studies were important, and while three quarters wished study of the target country to receive a lot of emphasis in an ideal course, less than half would include history or geography in this. Only 13% saw linguistics as a key area of study. The overwhelming emphasis, predictably, was on practical language skills.

The caricature that students traditionally learnt grammar and written language at school, register and spoken language during the year abroad, and little or nothing in three years of prose and translation classes incidentally receives some further support from studies of the impact of the year abroad on students' language skills that Dr Meara's report includes.

* * *

David Nott, looking at aims and objectives of modern language courses and how they may be met and evaluated, graphically stresses the changes in student population - and the concomitant differences in skills, attitudes, background and expectations - by pointing out that a greater percentage of young people are now entering *higher* education than were admitted to grammar schools only a generation or two ago. His chapter is placed first since it represents in many ways the starting point for the reflexions of the other contributors, each of which provides more than a merc case study by surveying methodological constructs as well as past and present practice in a particular field. To talk of aims, objectives and above all contracts will to some smack of the kind of narrow and unacademic commercialism which French Departments exist to counterbalance. But for others, they are a necessary step in replacing the sloppy thinking prevalent in a few modern language departments over recent decades with academic curricula that result not from tradition and inertia but from a detailed rethink of what a university education should seek to achieve. It is a significant sign of the times that the National Union of Students now advocates an individual learning contract for each student. David Nott's chapter, then, is of relevance to all of us: we may not agree with the conclusions, but to ask the questions is vital.

The need to adapt our grammar teaching to the new skills and attitudes our students bring from school and the world of work is recognised in the AFLS Grammar Initiative, coordinated, like the present series of books, by the AFLS Projects and Publications Committee. The Grammar Initiative, an attempt to spread good ideas and good practice, and to counter the tendency to institutional competition by encouraging open collaboration, arose from workshops held at Newcastle University and at Birkbeck College devoted to the issue of the grammatical competence of students entering French departments. Four groups, representing a score of different institutions, adopted different practical approaches - grammar-brochures, grammar based on authentic written texts, communicative grammar, and *Vidéogrammaire*: the results are now being made available free of charge (with the exception of the video) to AFLS members.

* * *

Small wonder, given the trends in student demand, that universities may seek to appoint trained and competent language teachers with a research interest in the language field. Nor can such responses to movements in student interest be dismissed as some kind of thatcherite embracing of philistine market forces. University language syllabuses have for generations been staff-centred, reflecting the sometimes obscure research interests of those colleagues brought together by a (frequently politically-determined) appointments policy undermined by the serendipity of staff movements and early retirements. University conferences, even on language learning, have often centred on the staff experience not the student one. Student-centred curricula need not - must not - be a pick-and-mix assortment reflecting no more than passing fashion and incoherent adolescent fancies. They must, rather, reflect those skills, competences and personal development which are the objectives of a university education, and those activities and areas of knowledge which can demonstrably deliver them. For decades, staff research has dictated student curricula. Perhaps it is time that student needs influenced staff research.

To adopt an optimistic outlook, there may be in all this a pointer to future changes in the profile of university language teachers, as the generation first employed in the expansion of the 1960s moves to retirement, as financial credits follow student choices along modularised pathways, and as the whole expanded university network embraces a quality assurance system which incorporates appraisal, classroom inspections and staff development opportunities. We may hope that bad classroom practice will progressively be eliminated, and we are likely to see a trained and professionally competent population of language teachers, many of whom will also pursue research in a linguistic or applied-linguistic domain.

But this will not happen tomorrow. A combination of vested interests and financial pressures is increasing the number of language teachers on temporary and part-time contracts. Adequate training is not always available. One year's full-time training is required before you may be allowed to teach language in schools: is effective university language teaching really less demanding? Or do we possess innate skills denied to mere schoolteachers?

Those with interest and expertise in effective language learning have too often failed to ensure that such expert knowledge penetrates university language departments - even adjacent ones. It is an open secret that some of the most internationally distinguished departments of Linguistics or Education in the United Kingdom are allied with some of the least well-informed Modern Language departments, often sharing a name or even a corridor but not sharing research findings and good practice in language teaching. Theoretical linguists even within modern language departments are not necessarily the best teachers. And as long as certain applied linguists refer to language teaching "practitioners" as if to a separate and probably lower species, deploring the gulf that exists but failing to build bridges, the effectiveness and status of university language teaching remain uncertain. The administrative divisions which have often separated the different language specialists into watertight compartments labelled EFL, French and German are no doubt also partly responsible for the slow spread of information and good practice across higher education language teaching.

New developments must also alter the shape of the language classroom: as professionals, we should ensure that, in the face of the uncomfortable but irresistible determinants of increasing student numbers and decreasing resources, teaching strategies are dictated by knowledge of which activities effectively promote linguistic and other competences. We must continue to research, document and publicise the real costs of successful language learning. Otherwise, there is a danger that the myth promoted even by some within language departments - namely, that language teaching is a straightforward, mechanical process for which no training is required and which is adequately carried out by untrained native-speakers or cheap part-timers, supported by machines which are capital-intensive rather than labour-intensive - might be used to justify the worst excesses.

* * *

Geneviève Parkes in her article refers to the potential conflict between teaching and research, and the recent Research Assessment Exercise has certainly marked differences in mission between institutions, particularly across the old binary line. This is not the place to pursue in greater depth the issue of research in the field(s) of modern languages, but the Research Assessment Exercise has once again underlined the mismatch between the areas which university staff are researching (and in which they are supervising research students) and the teaching needs of undergraduates. Common sense suggests that new academic staff should come from the ranks of research students. But analysis of Research Assessment data for French shows that only 8% of current language postgraduates are researching in the applied language area, in which more than half the job vacancies have occurred over the past twelve months. The survey by Gareth Thomas of likely appointments over the next three years reinforces the mismatch: there are predicted to be 56 jobs in area/media studies, 44 in business studies, 31 in literary studies, and 130 in linguistics and applied language. Thomas concludes: "it is hard to see where the new staff are to be recruited, since we are not producing postgraduate students in any numbers in these areas"[13], and that "research has acquired an autonomous existence and is not driven entirely by the requirements to staff certain areas of growth"[14]. This mismatch has long been evident[15], but the nettle remains ungrasped.

Perhaps a suspicion of practical outcomes is endemic among humanities lecturers. University teachers in the humanities certainly appear allergic to the word "training". In a survey of *THES* readers, reported in January 1993, humanities alone of all the subject groups in UK higher education believed (by

47% to 34%) that "it is not the purpose of a university to train people for jobs". Is there really a contradiction in expecting students to acquire the professional skills the country needs while also accomplishing their personal and intellectual development? The fallout of successive Research Assessment Exercises may be to widen still further the gap between teaching and research, to the extent that the very notion of the teacher-researcher may be abandoned, although this would call into question the whole meaning of the word university.

Many academics, including the present editors, believe intensely in the ideal of the teacher-researcher, whose own commitment to advancing the twin causes of truth and knowledge is transmitted to learners along with her subject expertise, and whose teaching never allows her to forget that it is the student experience which is central to the institution we call a university. The demographic profile of modern language teachers in British universities and colleges gives us now a unique chance to redefine our priorities as professionals. We hope that the present collection of articles will provide material for reflection as we discuss the possible creation of a single over-arching body to represent the whole modern languages sector.

* * *

The year abroad, which an overwhelming majority of modern language teachers see as an absolutely essential part of a degree programme, may be coming under threat from fast-track degrees, cost-cutting and a sudden brake on expansion of student numbers. As Ben Fisher recalls, it used to be different: in the 1960s, in many universities, the model was very simple. Students were appointed as assistants, were sent off to France knowing nothing, and returned having done nothing - at least in the academic sphere. One of the present editors went to France in October 1968, vaguely aware that there had been some troubles earlier in the year, but wholly ignorant of what the issues might have been, just as no guidance had been provided on how to find accommodation or how to open a bank account: things have improved since, with a clearer acknowledgment on the part of staff of what they owe to their students. The survey by Peter Dyson in the 1980s demonstrated the value of the year abroad, and although practice is still very uneven across institutions, most will usually give the choice of an assistantship, a student exchange or a work placement; the student will go to France with a good knowledge of its culture, institutions and society; a handbook will provide an introduction to the local circumstances; two visits a year from the home institution and supervision by a local academic will ensure maximum benefit from the stay abroad; and the concrete result will be a project and/or dissertation linked to the area of residence. Gordon Inkster reviews the range of issues raised by the year abroad - arguably the most ambitious piece of self-directed learning any of our students undertake. The chapter by Ana Barro and Hanns Grimm advances still further the preparation for the year abroad, its integration into the overall degree programme, and therefore, arguably, its value to the learner. The report on the TVU experience shows how wrong is the assumption that French, after EFL, has the monopoly of new developments. When new approaches are implemented initially within other language studies, it is right that innovations of such broad potential should be included in a collection such as this.

Many of the other themes touched on in this overview of some of the contextual issues receive fuller treatment in the book itself. Testing, for example, is arguably one of the keys to the future of modern languages, and is covered by Phil Powrie and David Nott, as well as by Marie-Christine Press who recalls learners' demand for nationally recognised certificates. Whether, in institution-wide language programmes, these end up being NVQ's or an alternative, there is no doubting the huge and urgent demand. Modularisation, in turn, will place new demands on language testing: rather than waiting to test exit velocity after four years of study, universities will need to attach credits to semester-length modules, and to specify more precisely than ever before exactly what level a student has reached in the range of language skills. Powrie's concern to define aims and criteria will inevitably become universal.

For Michèle Dickson, a learner-centred approach is fundamental for defining the authentic materials used in the classroom. The view is shared by Nigel Armstrong and Geoffrey Hare, who extend the concept into the area of sociocultural competence, examining the target-audience dimension in writing tasks, and the nature of authenticity itself. It is in this context that Armstrong and Hare look at the integration of literature, which is the central theme of Margaret Parry's article. Several authors look at the skills provided by language courses over and above the purely linguistic.

The integration of new technology, unsurprisingly, receives broad coverage from differing practical perspectives, especially in the articles by Michael Glencross, Ben Fisher, and Chris Emery, though video is of concern also to Phil Powrie. Emery leaves no doubt that there are no simplistic answers when it comes to multimedia, or indeed about the teaching and learning process itself - a warning echoed by Michèle Dickson. There are no simplistic answers either when it comes to self-access learning: here it is Marie-Christine Press whose views are echoed by Emery and by Nott. While Gordon Inkster, Ana Barro and Hanns Grimm stress the complexity of issues related to the year abroad, Geneviève Parkes looks at the other side of the coin - the use that can be made of native speakers on ERASMUS and LINGUA exchanges in the UK.

Geneviève Parkes' humorously written but essentially serious tailpiece reflects on the compartmentalisation of French studies and the status of language teachers within it. She poses the problems of *real* integration, and makes clear how regarding language skills as divorced from the rest of the curriculum can be counter-productive. She looks at *horizontal* integration as a response to problems of motivation and effective teaching, problems addressed in a different context and a different style by Marie-Christine Press, whose chapter on learner autonomy and self-access learning covers many basics which may be unfamiliar to a good number of readers, as well as providing practical exemplification, a virtue shared by several articles, including Michèle Dickson's chapter on teaching language for special purposes.

The whole book provides, we hope, rich food for thought and a challenge to complacency: this, as well as supporting innovation, and providing discussion topics in staff rooms, is in part the mission of the whole AFLS series. We additionally hope that, as pressure to publish increases, if colleagues know there is a likely refereed outlet for reports on sound teaching initiatives, they - and the rest of their Department - may be more willing to undertake new ventures in the language classroom. Furthermore, there is a need for an outlet for *younger* voices, reflecting on what French Studies means in the 1990s and beyond.

The next volume in this AFLS/CILT series, *Discourse Variety in Contemporary French: descriptive and pedagogical approaches*, will contain contributions both from the best established names in the field and from research students: in the hope that such books will continue to provide a forum for professional discussion among university linguists, both editors and contributors welcome feedback from readers.

James A. Coleman,   Annie Rouxeville,
University of Portsmouth   University of Sheffield

Nota Bene. With regard to gender-specific pronouns and possessives, solutions adopted are the responsibility of the individual author.

Notes

1. Gareth Thomas, *Survey of European Languages in the United Kingdom*, London, CNAA, 1993, p.13. The survey covers 40 universities or university colleges from each of the former UFC and PCFC sectors - 101 respondents in all across five languages. It shows that of over 53,000 students of languages, some 29,000 are not regarded as "specialist linguists".

2. Gareth Thomas, *op. cit.*, p.36.

3. For example, "Quality in a university or of a university has little or nothing to do with management. It has to do with the professional excellence of individuals as teachers and researchers." Letter to *Times Higher Educational Supplement*, January 8 1993.

4. Macdonald Daly, *The Times Higher Education Supplement*, December 13 1991, p.16.

5. *Ibid.*, quoting the Cox report on English in schools.

6. *Times Higher Educational Supplement* editorial, October 18 1991, p.12.

7. Malcolm Smith et al, *The Right Angle: Your Degree in French*, Runnymede Books, 1987, p.7.

8. Linda Hantrais, *The Undergraduate's Guide to Studying Languages*, CILT, 1989, p.20.

9. James A. Coleman and Gabrielle Parker, eds., *French and the Enterprise Path: developing transferable and professional skills*, London, AFLS/CILT, 1992. See the Introduction, especially pp.10 and 12-13; Gabrielle Parker, *op. cit.*, pp.29-42; and also, for instance, James A. Coleman, "Project-based learning, transferable skills, information technology and video", *Language Learning Journal* 5 (March 1992), pp.35-7.

10. G.E. Hare & P. Powrie, "Developing Transferable Personal Skills in a Business Studies Option of a French Undergraduate Degree", in J.A. Coleman & Gabrielle Parker (eds.), *op. cit.*, pp.63-80, especially pp.64-5.

11. Richard Towell and Jane Hanstock, "Introducing Enterprise into the Teaching of French in Higher Education", in J.A. Coleman & Gabrielle Parker (eds.), *op. cit.*, pp.81-99, especially pp.82-3.

12. A pilot questionnaire administered in January 1993 to 30 attenders at workshops devoted to the teaching and assessment of written skills elicited the fact that, although all were involved in language testing at the highest level, only one could name the obvious research journal in language testing, and none could name a book devoted to the topic. Only one in six knew that BAAL stood for the British Association for Applied Linguistics - a clear indicator of the thickness of the walls that remain to be broken down between specialist disciplines.

The AFLS AGM in September 1992 agreed to a national research initiative, based on the successful Grammar Initiative described in this Introduction, in the fields of language testing and the effects of instruction on learning and acquisition. There will be papers at the Aix-en-Provence AFLS conference in September 1993, contributions to the Portsmouth University conference on University Language Testing in April 1994, and the twin themes of the September 1994 AFLS conference at Southampton University will again be testing and the effects of instruction.

13. Gareth Thomas, *Survey of European Languages in the United Kingdom*, London, CNAA, 1993, p.46.

14. *Op. cit.*, p.66

15. See for example the article "French with Tears" by Anthony Lodge, *The Times Higher Education Supplement*, February 7 1992, p.16.

Towards Integration in French Studies

David Nott, Lancaster University

Note: Some of the material in this chapter is adapted from a four-page discussion paper, "Delivering the Modern Languages Curriculum", prepared for the Department of Modern Languages, Lancaster University, in February 1992.

In this chapter, I propose to examine some of the criteria involved in the establishment of an integrated programme of undergraduate studies in French. Although several references will be made to the first-year French language course at Lancaster University, the suggestions as to Aims, Objectives, Syllabuses and Processes cover the degree course in French as a whole, and the issues raised must be of concern to all those involved in university French teaching.

The Local Context

All undergraduate students at Lancaster study three subjects to Part I level in their first year. All students follow the same first-year course in French Studies, whether they are intending to study Part II French for three years as a Single Major or Combined Major subject, for one to three years as a Minor subject, or not at all. Numbers of students following the first-year course in French Studies increased from 93 in 1988/89 to 123 in 1991/92.

This system offers obvious advantages to all students in terms of flexibility and freedom of choice within a clear and coherent framework. The first year course in French Studies provides the opportunity to mix and study, for three hours of each week, in fairly small groups (at present, 12 - 13) with fellow-students following a wide variety of Part I subject combinations, and with an equally wide range of intended subjects and combinations for Part II. At a stage when many students' view of themselves, the world and their place in it, and their capacity to cope with these, undergo significant changes, in most cases for the better, there is much to be said for a system that enables them to work closely with the full range of people who have chosen to study French, and to see for themselves the wide variety of reasons why people do so, instead of looking out on other species of first year students from within the confines of a narrow group of like-minded people, such as Single Major "specialists" or "Management subjects" students.

1. Students

A degree course in French designed before 1987, when just over one in seven of the age group went on to higher education, is unlikely to be wholly appropriate after 1992 when, for the first time, over one in four of the age group entered higher education, i.e. a higher proportion than those of their parents and grand-parents in England and Wales who, at the age of eleven, were deemed suitable for grammar school education. As a result of social, cultural, technological and economic changes, many skills, attitudes and expectations which were once taken for granted of entrants to higher education have been modified, or replaced by other values: wisdom and credibility are associated more with the street than with the campus. Our own aims thus require careful reassessment and redefinition: what do we think these students should learn while they are with us, and how, and why?

In French Studies, post-A level and Highers students are, on the whole, increasingly at ease in speaking and understanding the language, but less aware of grammatical categories and terminology; their experience of reading French literature, and of thinking, speaking and writing about it, may be minimal or non-existent. More importantly, they may be unused to techniques such as preparing work for small group activities, speaking continuously from notes, working on their own or in a group-led rather than a teacher-dominated environment.

If due account is not taken of these changes when designing the syllabus for the first year onwards, students may find themselves unable, or even unwilling, to derive the full benefit from activities which are, in themselves, pedagogically sound and educationally worthwhile. For example, when, at Lancaster, a system of assessed oral *exposés*, to be given in front of each final year student's French language class, was introduced in 1985-86, a staff-student meeting had to be called, at which I attempted to quell students' concern and even indignation, at the idea of having to speak French in front of their peers. Subsequently a system of individual or group oral *exposés* was introduced throughout the course, so that every student has to make an assessed presentation in each of the nine terms of years 1, 2 and 4. Apart from token expressions of alarm and reluctance when this system is explained to UCCA candidates and during the introductory talk for first-year students, it is now a thoroughly accepted part of the course.

2. Aims

Although there are many and varied reasons why students choose to follow a degree course in French, their individual aims and expectations may at first be only dimly formulated, and, in many cases, change during the first year of study. In addition, one can observe from students' responses to annual feedback questionnaires (see **6. Evaluation**) that these changes are influenced as much by the actual modes of learning and teaching (see **5. Processes**) as by stated objectives or syllabuses.

If, as experience suggests, there is some degree of hiatus, or even of mismatch, between (a) what new students think they want, and are going to get, from a French Studies course and (b) what we observe that they gain from it, then the formulation of an explicit set of *aims* for the course becomes a delicate matter: we ourselves need to be clear as to our aims in devising and running the course - but when, in what form, and by what means, should new and prospective students be informed of our aims for them? UCCA candidates reading prospectuses are best served by a clear and sober presentation of the structure and content of French courses: it is on the basis of these that they are likely to make their choices, rather than on a generalised and perhaps inflated statement of aims and claims. If we provide new first-year students with a set of aims, we need to make clear that most of these are intended to cover the full four year period; we also need to show, at the start of work on each component of the first-year course, how it can be made to serve some or all of these aims. Perhaps the best place for a statement of Aims is as a preamble to the statement of Objectives for each part of the course. A set of aims for the French Studies course as a whole could include the following points:

Educational aims   - to contribute to each student's personal, social and cognitive development;
- to make each student more articulate in both English and French.

Cultural aims   - to further each student's awareness and appreciation of francophone culture, including historical, social, economic and artistic dimensions;
- to encourage and enable each student to adopt a bicultural (British and francophone) approach, in every area of the course.

Vocational aims   - to help each student to develop the social skills needed in order to function effectively in positions of responsibility at work.

In drawing up this set of aims, I have assumed that they would apply to every category of student following a degree course in French Studies; indeed, it would be difficult to imagine a category of student to which any of these aims should not apply.

In each of the three spheres (educational, cultural, vocational) these aims include the development of what, for want of a better phrase, one might call *bicultural competence*. Far from requiring students to renounce or neglect their own cultural and linguistic heritage so that they end up knowing more about the francophone world than about their own, the French Studies course should be explicitly directed towards students' parallel development in the two languages and cultures, by constant cross-reference between then at every stage. In this way students' own cultural background can provide a fruitful point of comparison, in each area of the course, for their growing awareness of francophone culture (this point is exemplified in **3. Objectives**). If the development of bicultural competence is accepted as our aim, it also follows that some of the work on the French course should be done in English (see **5. Processes**).

3. Objectives

For a degree course in French to fulfil educational, cultural and vocational *aims* such as those outlined above, specific *objectives* need to be formulated, more explicitly than in the past.

If a list of objectives is presented to students at the start of their first year it can be drawn up in the form of a contract between the French section or department and the student (a contract along these lines was recently drafted by the German Studies section at Lancaster University). Presenting the objectives of the course in this form has a double advantage: (a) it reminds teaching staff (full-time, part-time and lecteurs) that little can be taken for granted in terms of students' awareness of the links between the things we ask them to do and what they themselves want to gain from the course; and (b) it reminds students that, while it is our responsibility to know what we are teaching, how to deliver it, and why, it is their responsibility to participate and collaborate, with open eyes and minds, in the learning process.

Drawing up a set of objectives involves looking separately at things which, in practice, are carried out in combination. Few learning activities, particularly at degree level, are limited to a single objective. Indeed, one advantage of a set of specific objectives is that the purpose of a particular task can be shown to be more broadly and/or more deeply based that the mere accomplishment of the task itself.

Objectives for the French Studies course fall under three principal headings: communication, culture and cognition; these can be seen as a pyramid with cognition at the apex, since that is what higher education may be said to be ultimately about; all three are interdependent, all three are involved in all years of the course, all three, one might hope, come into play during every teaching hour.

When classifying objectives for the degree course, the most economical and coherent form of presentation is probably under two headings, *skills* and *knowledge*, so long as it is understood that skills without knowledge can only be an empty shell, and that knowledge without skills is a sterile core. In the field of French Studies, for example, it would be particularly unfortunate, and debilitating for all concerned, if degree courses were to be conceived, devised, organised and assessed as two distinct and separate halves, with "language" providing the skills and "literature/institutions" providing the knowledge (see **4. Syllabuses** and **5. Processes**).

Some possible points for inclusion in a list of objectives for the French Studies course as a whole are given below; skills and knowledge concerning the English language and British culture appear as explicit objectives:

Skills   - to communicate effectively in French (speaking and understanding) with educated native speakers of differing age, status and profession, in situations ranging from informal conversation to a formal interview or presentation;
- to read and understand without assistance a non-technical article in French from a serious newspaper or magazine;
- to read for enjoyment a medium-length novel, or similar work, in French;
- to compose and write in French thoughtful, coherent, and convincing reports, summaries, discussion papers, articles and other items;
- to write creative/imaginative pieces in French, e.g. letters, stories, diaries, pastiches, for personal enjoyment and the entertainment of others;
- to communicate effectively in English, in speech and writing, in social and professional contexts, with native speakers of English;
- to communicate effectively in English, in social and professional contexts, with non-native speakers of English.

Knowledge - to have a sufficiently wide-ranging awareness of literature, the arts and other aspects of the culture of francophone countries, to be able to sustain general conversations and discussions, in French or in English, with educated French speakers;
- to be aware of major issues of current concern, and their background, in francophone countries, in social and economic affairs, politics and institutions, for example;
- to have developed a personal interest in, and appreciation of, at least two topics, individuals or works in any area of the literature or the arts of francophone countries;
- to further their knowledge of British history and culture, and to reappraise them in the light of their experience of francophone culture;
- to have analysed selected aspects of their personal experience, and of British culture, and to have formulated and articulated ideas about these, so as to be able to sustain conversation or discussions about them, in English or French, with educated French speakers;
- to be aware of important socio-situational variations in French usage, and of French speakers' attitudes to these;
- to have a knowledge of both English and French grammatical terminology, and of the salient differences, in terms of

pronunciation, spelling, meaning, vocabulary and syntax, between English and French;
- to be aware of the main features of English language and usage which cause difficulties of comprehension and production for French speakers.

French nationals, "bilingual" students, etc.

As credit transfer in higher education becomes a reality in Europe, a significant minority of students on French degree courses in Britain will have been French-speaking for all or part of their life. Arithmetically, the British degree system has always been able to cope with these students, balancing out marks lost in translation and marks gained in oral tests, and so on; nevertheless, courses, objectives and assessment schemes are traditionally based on the assumption that French is a foreign language for all students on the course. In most French sections or departments, the relatively small number of students with a French-speaking background makes it impractical to devise, teach and assess a separate course for them, and in any case, one may doubt whether separate provision would constitute a defensible manifestation of European integration. A set of demonstrably *bicultural* objectives for the French Studies course would enable equally coherent and challenging targets to be set for all students, whatever their origin - provided that syllabuses, learning and teaching modes, and schemes of assessment were in conformity with these objectives.

4. Syllabuses

If it consists of no more than a list of grammar points to be learnt, or of books to be studied, a syllabus raises more questions than it answers - about the methods, scope and depth of study, about the organisation and form of oral and written activities, including assessment, and about its relevance to the aims and objectives of the course as a whole.

The search, in some French departments, for more satisfactory definitions of a syllabus for language work, for example, has led to the existence of a number of disparate, even conflicting approaches: on the one hand, final year courses on culture/ institutions taught and assessed entirely in French, or second year courses where the acquisition and reinforcement of linguistic skills take place only as part of the performance of a set of tasks relating to a whole term's or whole year's topic; on the other hand, a series of translation classes, or essay classes with the *lecteur*.

A more general trend, influenced in part by changes in school syllabuses and methods, and by published teaching materials, has been towards topic-based language work, particularly in the first year.

Although a list of topics cannot constitute a syllabus it can provide a convenient focus, for periods of two to four weeks, for a set of language-learning activities. Some idea of the nature of these in the first year course at Lancaster may be gained from a brief account of the works covered in the last fortnight of Term 1, around the topic *Paris et le rôle de Paris*:

Materials - 3 printed texts for private study and exploitation in class: (a) extract from Zola, *Au Bonheur des Dames* (1883): les grands magasins; (b) extract from M. Winock (*Chronique des années 1960* (1987): "Les années en béton"; (c) article "Un TGV nommé désir" from *Libération* (1990): asking the pertinent question "Dans quel sens roulent les TGV?" (i.e. Paris-province or province-Paris);
- 1 audio and 1 video extract, with worksheets and transcripts;
- 1 film on a subject loosely related to the topic, e.g. Luc Besson, *Subway* (1985).

Lectures - 1 lecture in French on Paris;
- 1 lecture in English on grammar points arising from the 3 texts.

Classes - 2 language classes (with tutor); normally: activities on and around 1 or 2 of the 3 texts; other language work, depending on the tutor and the class; this time: second set of students' assessed oral *exposés* (4-5 minutes) on "Ma région";
- 2 classes (with **lectrice**): 1 "Pratique orale" (activites around one of the texts, or a text or topic suggested by the *lectrice*); 1 video class: work on extracts from French TV (news or documentary).

Assessment   - oral *exposé* (see above);
- normally: fortnightly language laboratory hour (open access with self-correcting exercises); this time: end of term aural/translation/vocabulary test;
- 1 piece of assessed written work, generally arising from the current or the previous fortnight's topic.

Other lectures and classes
> - 1 history lecture, 2 literature lectures, 2 literature classes.

As can be seen, the first year course is expensive in staff time; it is not at all certain that contact hours, class sizes and assessment tasks will remain at their present level in years to come.

Perhaps the most convincing argument in favour of a topic-based syllabus for language work is that, as suggested in 3. above, skills without knowledge are an empty shell; a *skills-based* course needs also to be *content-centred*. In life, work and study it is normally best, if one is speaking or writing, to have something to speak or write about. In the context of learning a foreign language, it is clear from research evidence that linguistic skills are best developed through frequent and *meaningful* contacts with the foreign language. Which leads us to the crucial issue, that of: what are the modes of learning, teaching and assessment which are most likely to make students' encounters with the French language meaningful to them?

5. Processes

Increasing pressure of student numbers is likely to lead French departments and sections to seek (a) to revise the allocation of time between independent study, lectures to the whole year-group, classes, seminars and individual tutorials and (b) to re-evaluate modes of learning and teaching (e.g. the content of lectures and activities in classes/seminars) in the light of agreed objectives. Awkward questions will need to be asked, and difficult decisions taken, in respect of courses or course components which were considered appropriate or even innovatory, twenty years ago, but which would stand less chance of passing the scrutiny of departmental and faculty committees if they were being presented for approval as new courses today.

In the rest of this section, four aspects of the learning/ teaching process are considered separately: Independent study; Classes; Lectures; and Assessment.

Independent study: For reasons outlined earlier (see **1. Students**), simply increasing the amount of time which is deemed to be spent on independent study, in order to make necessary savings in contact hours, is unlikely to be productive in terms of students' commitment or achievement. For all components of the course, students need to be given explicit and detailed guidance, both initially and at appropriate points thereafter, in techniques of independent study, including how to evaluate and revise one's study methods. In particular, students need guidance and support in the matter of *preparation* for classes and seminars: they should certainly come to classes with an open mind, but not with a blank mind and an empty notebook, simply expecting to be edified and/or entertained by the tutor. If the class is conducted, at least for part of the time, as a forum to which students can bring their ideas, problems and solutions, which they then exchange among themselves and with the tutor, their preparation will be seen to have a point and to be acknowledged. In fifty minutes, sitting with anything from ten to twenty others, students cannot expect their preparation to be covered exhaustively: it can only be sampled; but if, for one reason or another, it is wholly ignored by the tutor, the pedagogical life-line feeding independent study will have been cut off.

Classes and seminars are expensive in terms of staff time: it would be a salutary planning exercise to establish (a) which components, aspects, processes etc, of the French Studies course can be delivered via independent study or lectures (see below) and (b) which ones can *only* be served by work in groups. In a word, what are classes for? Pedagogical techniques involving pair and group work, and other forms of structural activity, are widely used at the secondary level with classes of up to thirty; sensitively adapted for under-graduate use, these techniques can help to ensure that all students participate actively, as listeners and as speakers, in the class. A regular class, twice a week, with the same students but alternating between tutor and lecteur, can provide focus and continuity - a welcome change from independent study and the distance and anonymity of the lecture hall.

All course descriptions given out to students could include details of the nature and purpose of activities proposed for classes/seminars; for example, the use of English and/or French as a means of communication (and the reasons for each), the types and approximate amount of student preparation, the use to be made of informal and formal contributions, exercises, presentations and reports, and the opportunities for discussion and participation. Closer definition of class activities might also enable particular roles to be assigned to students with a French-speaking background, for example in classes conducted by *lecteurs*.

Even more expensive than class time, and even more appreciated by students, is the opportunity for individual tutorial sessions, even if they are of only ten to fifteen minutes' duration. One way of providing for this is to set aside certain weeks within the scheduled timetable, for example around the time when a major coursework assignment is set, and/or when it is returned to the student.

Lectures constitute the traditional backbone of a degree course, and a significant corpus of research into lecturing now exists. It is of course possible to obtain a degree without attending a single lecture, whether from choice (following a distance-learning programme) or necessity (French students working in schools as *surveillants* and relying on *cours polycopiés*). Such a system, applied to the majority of students, would surely constitute an impoverishment of their education, but it does suggest that lecturers might avoid using lecture time for conveying the kinds of information which are readily available in books, or can be distributed in the form of duplicated handouts, including short lists of French words and phrases. Bibliographies, where appropriate, could consist of brief comments (e.g. on the level of difficulty, the author's perspective) on a limited number of books, together with chapter/page references to relevant sections. Many lectures could help to demonstrate recommended techniques of study through the step-by-step analysis of a small number of sample issues, extracts, points of language, etc. instead of general surveys.

For students, lectures present them with an invidious choice; whether to concentrate on everything that is being said (or presented in other forms) or to take notes, at the risk of missing the next point or vital link in the lecturer's argument. This dilemma is particularly acute in the case of lectures given in French. Lecturers can use a number of techniques to alleviate matters: pauses after particularly important points, to enable notes to be taken; variations of tone and pace which signal the relative importance of what is being said; indicating, each time visual aids are used, whether the information is or will be also available in handout form; providing one or two short breaks, in the course of a 50-minute lecture, to allow for physical and mental relaxation, discussion, chat, daydreaming. In our own professional sphere, conference papers are commonly limited to 20 or 30 minutes, for reasons not directly connected with participants' comfort, but nevertheless with beneficial effects on their concentration.

Assessment: For staff and students alike, assessment is at the focal point of the learning and teaching process: a cumulative, and then a final verdict on years of work. If the assessment of course work is part of the system, it plays a vital role, readily accepted by most staff and students, in providing motivation through a series of definite goals, giving timely feedback on the success or otherwise of teaching and learning methods, and moderating - without removing - the pressures of the final examination. The drawback, however, is that course work assessment tends to be treated as part of the examination system: since each piece of work is given a mark that will count towards the final degree, its value as part of the learning process is liable to be neglected by students; this can have a knock-on effect on preparation for classes (see above, **Independent study**), which can be devalued in students' eyes because it appears to bring no immediate, measurable reward (or sanction).

Since each French department or section has its own aims, traditions and practices, it would be neither feasible nor desirable to draw up a set of assessment criteria having general validity; nor is there space here to cover the full range of courses in French Studies. It might, however, be helpful to consider in some detail one area which in one shape or form is found in all French Studies courses, namely the oral *exposé*.

Oral exposés: It can be argued - and in some degree courses it is the practice - that the place of the assessment of spoken French is as an integral part of the work done during and/or at the end of each course or course component on sociocultural topics (history, literature, institutions, economics, etc.), rather than in a "(French) language (skills)" course. Not least among the arguments in favour of this practice is that it enables the principal criterion for assessment of students' linguistic competence to be that of *fitness for purpose* - a purpose defined in terms of the overall objectives of a particular course or component.

In contrast to this, assessment of the traditional oral examination, or of oral *exposés* forming part of a "language skills" course, can sometimes appear to students, and perhaps even to examiners, as a hit-or-miss affair, where the importance attached to factors such as personality or charm, or idiosyncracies of pronunciation or grammar, may vary according to the personality and prejudices of individual examiners. Furthermore, it is extremely difficult for any tutor or examiner to apply half-a-dozen or more criteria simultaneously, within the space of 20 or 30 minutes. In practice, tutors can be provided with a check-list of points which they might study beforehand, and refer to occasionally and selectively in order to come to a decision on the mark to be given in a particular case.

The following guidelines, adapted from a list of suggestions I made in January 1991 for the assessment of final-year students' achievement in their termly oral *exposé* (at Lancaster, all Single and Combined Major students in French follow a core "language skills" course, in which oral and written skills have equal weight for assessment purposes), graphically illuminates the difficulties of defining criteria for assessment, if these cannot be integrated with precise objectives and a defined syllabus for the course as a whole:

1   **Structure**: clarity, organisation, links, cumulation

2   **Perspective**: depth and sophistication of argument; relation of ideas/examples to student's views/experience/ reading

3   **Coverage**: small number of main points, well ordered/linked, with interesting observations/conclusions

4   **Communication**: clarity of articulation, use of notes as cues, maintenance of eye contact, use of voice

5   **Register**: use of language appropriate to a formal (*exposé*) situation

6   **Flexibility**: ability to switch to a less formal, more spontaneous mode, during questions/discussion

7   **Range**: vocabulary adequate for the subject; use of sentence-structure/linkage to express nuances

8   **Fluency**: ability to maintain momentum, recover from an error or a false start; delivery neither too rapid nor too slow

9   **Authenticity**: pronunciation, intonation, stress patterns

10   **Accuracy**: e.g. use of tenses with *quand/si/pendant/depuis*; verb constructions + noun/infinitive; correct use of *faux amis*

The assessment of oral *exposés* (with or without guidelines such as those given above), and also of "the (French) (language) essay" throws into sharp relief the question of the relative importance of "content" versus "language" in a skills-based course. In the case of both *exposés* and essays, students may, even at the Finals stage, labour under the misapprehension that in a language test, "it doesn't matter what you say, as long as you get the French right". For what it is worth, I offer the following rule-of-thumb, which I have found to be equally applicable when assessing both *exposés* and essays: if I find myself concentrating on *what* is being said or written, then it is likely that the eventual grade will be above 60% (II 1 or better); if I find I am focussing on *expression*, then the eventual grade is likely to be below 60% (II 2 or lower).

Conversely, if the syllabus for sociocultural components of the course provides for all or some of the essays (course work or examination, or both) to be written in French, the "content versus expression" dilemma, for students and examiners, need not arise at all. Essays on history, literature, institutions, economics, etc. can be assessed according to exactly the same criteria, whether they are in English or in French, i.e. there will be no "marks off for inaccuracies" in the case of essays in French. Knowing this gives students the confidence to concentrate first and foremost on formulating, organising and linking their ideas in a coherent whole, and then, once the whole essay has been written, making a thorough check for accuracy in spelling, grammar, style and punctuation, in the same way as (one hopes) they do for essays written in English.

6. Evaluation

In an academic discipline such as French Studies, where in recent years so much has changed, *en amont* and *en aval*, not to mention within the discipline itself and among students, it is important to check that assessment methods are in line with course objectives and teaching methods. This calls not only for an annual review,in the light of student performance, of all examination papers and components, but also for the formulation of defined criteria for the awarding of marks, together with an analysis of the range and average level of marks awarded in previous years.

Similarly, if a system of course work assessment is included in the French Studies course, it is important to provide for a regular review, involving students as well as staff, covering the amount, frequency and types of assessed oral and written work set for all courses and components, and having particular regard to how different types of work are tackled by students, and whether each student is being set a sufficiently wide, varied, appropriate and challenging range of tasks.

Furthermore, the courses and course components themselves need to be reviewed regularly, both as regards their contribution to the value and coherence of the overall programme offered to students (fixed menu plus *à la carte* options), and the suitability of individual course components in terms of content, methods, work load, and so on. It goes without saying that students need to be involved in this process which means that student representatives have to be briefed about the nature and scope of the review in time for them to consult with their fellow students; the timing of this review within the academic year can be an awkward matter, particularly if one is to ensure that students are represented by some of those who have actually followed the most recent version of the courses or components being reviewed.

With the introduction of quality assessment and systems of appraisal, and a general increase in competition between and within universities for status, funds and students, student questionnaires are becoming part of the process of evaluation of individuals, courses and departments. While it is beyond the scope of this chapter to assess the usefulness of *staff*-centred student questionnaires in the appraisal of individual members of staff, it is worth pointing out that *course*-centred software for student feedback exists, and that carefully devised *course*-centred questionnaires can play a vital role in the evaluation of particular courses or course components. This form of questionnaire is especially suitable for courses which are taught by more than one member of staff: although students may have certain individuals in mind when making their responses, the impersonal nature of the exercise is conducive to frank and honest comments.

An example of a questionnaire used at Lancaster University is given as an Appendix to this chapter: the questions that appear are a slightly abridged version of the questionnaire on the 1991-92 French language course for first-year students, taught by six full-time staff, three part-time tutors and three *lectrices*.

A version of this questionnaire was used in each of the six years (1986-92) during which I was responsible for the first year language course; student responses constitute a major factor influencing the changes made in the course from year to year. As will be seen, the perspective of the questions is forward-looking, inviting collaborative and constructive participation on the part of the students. Their responses, whether positive or critical, are almost always framed in this spirit, as the following samples of answers to the final question will show:

> "Above all I enjoyed the variety that this year's course offered".
> (1987-88)
> "In general it is far too regimented - not enough freedom and spontaneity." (1987-88)
> "Very impressed - more language content than many courses, which was just what I wanted." (1987-88)

"No encouragement to speak better French." (1987-88)

"Well thought out. Don't change it except to make it all French-speaking." (1990-91)

"I've had 3 different language tutors this year and there was a large difference in their lessons - in amounts of Prep (*sic*) to do, amount of Oral spoken, etc. Should there be such a difference?" (1990-91)

"Very well-structured course." (1991-92)

"An enjoyable course. Not enough French spoken, I would like more lectures in French and more chance to have conversation in French." (1991-92)

"The course was hard work - my heaviest workload - but very interesting - good to cover many different topics." (1991-92)

Each year, some students end their questionnaire with an expression of thanks for the course. Whether these are justified or not, their expression is always welcome!

The way in which questionnaires are given out and collected, and above all the *timing* of the exercise, have a preponderant influence on the number of questionnaires returned:

Year	Date (approx)	Number returned
1986-87	late March	12
1987-88	mid April	56
1988-89	late April	35
1989-90	mid March	40
1990-91	late April	48
1991-92	late May	14

To achieve the highest rate of returns, the surest way is for group tutors to give out and collect in questionnaires during the same language hour, though this can have the drawback of producing some hasty comments. It is clearly unwise to leave the exercise until May, when students are becoming preoccupied with first year examinations.

7. Conclusion

Foreign language teaching is expensive in terms of staff time: it is not at all certain that contact hours, class sizes and assessment tasks can be maintained at present levels in years to come, either at Lancaster University or elsewhere. This is in itself a sufficient and pressing reason for a thorough reappraisal of students' skills and needs, of aims, objectives and syllabuses, of processes for teaching, learning and assessment, and of methods for evaluating the outcomes of the language courses we devise and teach. It is hoped that the present chapter will have made some practical contribution to this process.

------------------------------------   --

Appendix: Student questionnaire on the 1991-92 First Year French Language course at Lancaster University:

1   **TOPICS**

a Which topics and which texts did you like and find useful? Which did you not like?
b Suggest other topics and types of reading material you would recommend for next year.

2   **LANGUAGE WORK** (with tutors and lectrices)

a Which classwork activities did you find useful? Which not?
b Suggest other activities you would recommend for next year.

3   **GRAMMAR**

a (Booklets) Please make comments and suggestions as to the grammar examples, explanations and exercises.
b (Lectures) What additions or changes would you suggest for the programme of grammar lectures?

4   **COURSEWORK ASSESSMENT** (oral and written)

a In what ways did you find the three pieces of oral course work useful/not useful? Do you have any comments or suggestions for next year?
b Which types of written coursework did you find useful/not useful? Suggest other course work exercises you would find useful.

5 LECTURES IN FRENCH ON TOPICS

a Which topics for lectures did you like and find useful? Which not? Suggest other topics for lectures in French.

b In what ways did these lectures contribute to the course? Which features (presentation, handouts, amount of information, etc.) do you find most useful?

6 FEATURE FILMS

a Say which films you particularly liked/disliked, and why.

b Suggest films you think should be included in future. Should there be any films without subtitles?

7 LANGUAGE LABORATORY (audio and video)

a (Audio) The language lab classes will be unsupervised next year: exercises will be self-correcting, and the material tested in end-of-term "lab tests". Any comments/suggestions?

b (Video) Video classes next year will concentrate on news/ documentary TV extracts, and will be conducted by *lectrices* in the same groups as for language classes, so that each group will see "their" *lectrice* every week. Any comments/suggestions?

8 THE LANGUAGE COURSE AS A WHOLE

Please use this space for comments on this year's course, and suggestions for next year's course, that you have not made elsewhere.

Thank you for your cooperation in completing this questionnaire. If there are any points you would prefer to discuss with me personally, or with any other tutor, please do not hesitate to do so.

Integrating Word Processing into French Teaching in Higher Education

Michael Glencross,
University College of Ripon & York St. John

Many students of French in higher education have now had experience of working with computers since they were in school thanks to the increasing range of CALL software available[1]. The problem remains, however, of how to integrate this language learning aid into the curriculum so that IT in language teaching is more than just a set of permanently accessible but discrete programs which students are encouraged or required to sample in class contact time or, more likely, in their own time. One powerful remedy to this tendency towards fragmentation, a danger which seems to beset so many aspects of French as an area of study, lies in the creative use of word processing as a language learning tool. Word processing is for many students - and lecturers - the entry-level activity in working with computers but despite its unglamorous profile I want to demonstrate in this article its versatility as a language learning activity and to exemplify one way at least of making it an integral part of a semester-long course within a modular degree structure. My dual objective in planning this course component was, then, to develop students' written skills and confidence in one particular area of French, written language use, and to embed word processing as a teaching aid in the curriculum.

The first precondition for the successful integration of word processing into the teaching of French is linguistic. In the case where coursework and classwork is in French, which is increasingly the norm in higher education, it is essential for this component to be introduced into the curriculum in French. This entails therefore the use of the full French language version of the word processing software, rather than simply the English version supplemented by a French dictionary as an optional, add-on module. The software chosen in this case was Borland's *Sprint*. Whilst not widely used in this country especially in industry, *Sprint* is quite well known in France because of its cheap educational price and perhaps also because the company was founded by a Frenchman, Philippe Kahn. The software was used on a network of twenty PCs.

Using the French language version of the software immediately presents the students, even those with prior experience of word processing, with the opportunity and the challenge of acquiring the appropriate specialist vocabulary in French, the metalanguage of word processing. If the students are already familiar with the principle of menu-driven WP software all that is required is adjustment to the French terminology, so that they make the correct choices from the drop-down menus. In the case of students coming to word processing for the first time this process of familiarisation may take a little longer but is no different in nature. For reference purposes all students were given a list of the menu choices for basic operations but were encouraged in their own time to explore as fully as possible the facilities provided by the program. Explanations in French about the features available can also be accessed by students according to their requirements via help screens. This facility responds to individual needs and, like many aspects of IT, encourages independent student learning.

The menu choices of the software provide in themselves a rich and interesting source of linguistic material and show in particular the resources of the French language in creating a new technical vocabulary and the resourcefulness of the designers of the French version of the program[2]. The following list gives the choices from the main menu of the French version of *Sprint* with the terms from the English language version placed alongside:

Fichier	File
Editeur	Edit
Utilitaires	Insert
Caractères	Typestyle
Style	Style
Mise en page	Layout
Impression	Print
Gestion de fenêtres	Window
Outils	Utilities
Personnalisation	Customise

Terminé   Quit

A noticeable feature of the French terminology used here is that in every case except the last it uses a nominal form, whereas English with fewer morphological markers of the differences between nouns and verbs mixes nominal (six instances) and verbal (five instances) forms. This tendency towards nominalisation is a commonly remarked stylistic feature of French especially in technical registers. The pattern is confirmed by the comparison of the file menus of the two versions:

Nouveau fichier   New
Ouverture   Open
Fermeture   Close
Lecture et insertion   Insert
Sauvegarde   Save
Enregistrement sous   Write As
Abandon des modifications   Revert to Saved
Importation/Exportation   Translate
Gestion de fichiers   File Manager
Choix d'un fichier ouvert   Pick from List

More proof of the effort put into producing an authentically French rather than franglais version of the software can be found in these further examples taken from the menus or help screens with equivalent terms from the English language version of *Sprint* again set next to the French:

annulation d'effacement   undelete
bas de page   footer
basculer   toggle
biffure   strikethrough
césure   hyphenation
déplacement   move-cut
double frappe   double strike
écran d'aide   help screen
en-tête   header
exposant   superscript
fichier des secours   back-up file
interface utilisateur   user interface
indice   subscript
lancement   go

plein écran	zoom
police	font
rappel	insert/paste
règle de format	ruler
sauts de page	page break
surfrappe	overwrite
tri	arrange-sort
visualisation	screen preview

From a grammatical point of view we can again see the predominance of nominalisations in the French terminology but also worthy of note is the structure of the complex noun phrases which, except for the example *interface utilisateur*, deliberately avoid the franglais syntax of head noun and postmodifier without prepositions which is such a common feature of modern French syntax and which can lead to noun phrases of the type *corps panneaux particules, décor imitation pin*[3]. Our analysis of the terminology used in the software instructions shows clearly the ability of French to avoid English borrowings and calques in this area of new technology usually by assigning new meanings to existing lexical items[4].

The initial effort in familiarisation with the word processing software can then more properly be described as metalinguistic than linguistic in that it deals with the terminology specific to managing the facilities provided by *Sprint*. However, the main purpose of introducing this element into the curriculum is clearly linguistic, i.e. to improve students' productive skills in written French. Mastering the possibilities of the software in text-handling is not therefore an end in itself but simply a means to an end. To use French terminology, the *logiciel* is being transformed into *didacticiel*. In this way the aim becomes to use features of the software as language learning devices and to create exercises which exploit in as interesting a way as possible these possibilities.

The first set of exercises I want to present can be decribed as vocabulary-based as opposed to text-based. They exploit primarily the French word-lists built into the software either in the form of a simple dictionary for checking the spelling of words or a thesaurus of synonyms, two facilities standard to most word processing programs. Students can be asked to correct themselves a piece of text in French containing a number of spelling/typing errors and then check through it again using the spellcheck facility to see if there are further errors. In the case of French the very limitations of the spelling facilities (either "correction" or "vérification auto") which do not take account of semantic or syntactic factors[5] show up clearly the structure of the orthographic system and the nature of the distinctions between *phonogrammes*, *morphogrammes* and *logogrammes*, to use Nina Catach's terminology[6]. The inability of the software to correct errors can reinforce understanding of the structure and principles of the orthographic system. Thus, in a sentence such as "la reforme de l'orthographe du français est un sujet des plus controversées" neither *reforme* nor *controversées* will be corrected because they are possible forms, present in *Sprint*'s dictionary.

The synoynym dictionary is a richer resource but again its limitations can be put to pedagogic use. The following passage, adapted from an article in *Le Monde*, gives an example of such an exercise which is very easy to create:

*En vous servant du dictionnaire des synonymes de **Sprint**, à compléter, le cas échéant, par un dictionnaire français de type classique, remplacez chaque mot mis en relief dans le texte suivant par un synonyme:*

Les géants mondiaux de l'électronique grand public, les groupes néerlandais Philips et japonais Sony, ne *s'affronteront* pas sur le *champ clos* du son numérique. Déjà alliés dans le *domaine* du disque compact, ils ont décidé d'*étendre* leur accord de *coopération* à leurs derniers-nés, la cassette numérique, *mise au point* par la firme d'Eindhoven, et le minidisque compact réenregistrable, une *trouvaille* de la compagnie tokyote, deux produits hifi appelés, surtout le premier, à un très grand avenir. Philips s'est ainsi engagé envers son *partenaire* à *délivrer* avec lui des brevets sur la technologie du minidisque aux sociétés de matériel et de logiciel, de façon à *faciliter* le lancement à l'automne 1992 de ce nouveau support audio. En échange, Sony coopérera avec Philips pour introduire *en douceur* au printemps prochain les cassettes numériques compactes.

La sagesse *l'a* ainsi, une fois encore, *emporté*. Mais il semble que Philips sera le principal bénéficiaire de l'*opération*. Version *déclinée* du CD lancé en 1983, le minidisque devrait avoir, comme tel, plus de difficultés à *s'imposer* sur le marché. *En revanche*, comme le CD l'avait fait avec le 33 tours, la cassette numérique signe purement et simplement la *mort* à terme de la magnétocassette, vieille aujourd'hui de vingt-six ans. *Atout* majeur, elle sera *capable* de lire les vieilles cassettes. D'ores et déjà, cinquante-neuf firmes se sont engagées à *soutenir* la cassette numérique, Sony devient la soixantième.

In the majority of cases in this passage the synoynym dictionary of *Sprint* throws up an appropriate replacement term or set of terms. The interest of advanced learners should, however, be drawn to problem cases and to the examination of the cause of the problem. In the above passage the problematic terms are the following: *champ clos, mise au point, en douceur, l'a emporté, délivré, déclinée.* The difficulty posed by the first four exemples is that they are, wrongly, analysed in each case by the dictionary as discrete lexical items not as single units of meaning. Thus in the sentence "La sagesse *l'a* ainsi *emporté*" the dictionary picks up only the final term which is grammatically ambiguous and proposes as a replacement the adjectives *brutal/coléreux/fougueux/impulsif/vif.* In the other two instances the problem is semantic ambiguity. In most cases of polysemy the synonym dictionary makes appropriate distinctions of meaning but here it has not been programmed to take account of the sense of *délivrer* as in "délivrer un diplôme" not "délivrer un otage" nor *décliner* as in "décliner un produit" (= modifier)[7] instead of as in "décliner une offre".

To do a conventional synonym exercise of this type using the computer instead of pen and paper is only justifiable if the new medium has distinct advantages. In the present case this condition is fulfilled in a number of ways. Firstly students can access a synonym dictionary different in structure from a paper one, a dictionary which from the inflected form refers them to the root form or lemma and allows them to move rapidly between large numbers of lexical items, making connections between them. Secondly its method of operating including its shortcomings illustrates a number of features about the structure of the lexis of French. Thirdly it encourages rather than discourages use of a conventional synonym dictionary for comparison and as a complement. Finally it stimulates an open-ended approach to the exercise and allows flexibility between a collaborative or an individual approach to the exercise. Even with a piece of dedicated CALL software it would be difficult and very time-consuming to construct a synonym exercise such as the one illustrated which predicted all the acceptable or possible answers. Such exercises can be available to students within or outside class time by being downloaded from a master file on to the individual machines in the network. The students are then able to complete the exercises and print them but not to edit the original master files.

In a similar way word processing software can be used to create gapped exercises, for prediction of lexical items or grammatical forms from the context but in this case the advantages of dedicated CALL programs over the word processed version are clear: the former are able to provide help, feedback and correction for the responses of individual students[8]. However, whilst the word processed versions of such exercises are obviously less user-friendly and informative they can certainly be created far more quickly because there is no need to predict student responses, provide comments or produce distractors, features which make the creation of exercises via typical authoring programs so time-consuming. A good use of such an exercise would be for practising verb tenses, by replacing the infinitive with the correct tense and form of the verb.

After having examined the role of word processing software in creating exercises involving lexical or, in some cases, grammatical choices, I want now to turn to my second category, exercises which develop text-based language skills. This type of application of word processing to language learning draws attention to the importance of cohesion devices and coherence in language use. Instead of predicting an appropriate lexical item or grammatical form from the context, the student will typically be required to sequence correctly units of text[9]. The two most obvious units of text to use in such exercises are the grammatical unit of the sentence or the spatial unit of the line. An example of the former would generate the following jumbled text, taken again from a short two-paragraph article[10] in *Le Monde*:

> L'important est pour elles de bien choisir l'émission à parrainer et de ne pas réaliser des associations trop évidentes. Cette pratique, pourtant très coûteuse, est très prisée des grandes firmes. La mode en matière de communication est au sponsoring d'émissions de télévision.

> Les slogans publicitaires de cette marque de lunettes seront donc présents lors des retransmissions du championnat de France, de la Coupe de France, des Coupes d'Europe et des matchs de l'équipe de France espoirs. L'entreprise Alain Afflelou semble avoir compris ce principe puisqu'elle vient de signer un premier accord de partenariat de trois ans avec Canal+ concernant l'ensemble des matchs de football diffusés par la chaîne. Ils seront intégrés en début et en fin d'émission selon la technique du *billboard* (mise en scène du logo de la marque) mais aussi durant les matchs eux-mêmes (lors de mi-temps, durant les rappels des scores ou les ralentis) et dans les bandes annonces.

Resequencing the above passage depends on the recognition of the function of the following terms as linking devices: *cette pratique, pour elles, ce principe, cette marque de lunettes, Ils*. These examples are typical of the types of anaphora used in written French texts since they depend on grammatical reference (use of pronouns or determiners) or on semantic reference (use of synonyms or hyponyms)[11].

If, however, we jumble the original two paragraph text by complete line rather than by sentences we can generate, for example, the following passage:

L'important est pour elles de bien choisir l'émission
La mode en matière de communication est au sponsoring
très coûteuse, est très prisée des grandes firmes.
d'émissions de télévision. Cette pratique, pourtant
à parrainer et de ne pas réaliser des associations
trop évidentes.

lunettes seront donc présents lors des retransmissions
principe puisqu'elle vient de signer un premier accord
de partenariat de trois ans avec Canal+ concernant
L'entreprise Alain Afflelou semble avoir compris ce
l'ensemble des matchs de football diffusés par la
chaîne. Les slogans publicitaires de cette marque de
du championnat de France, de la Coupe de France, des
espoirs. Ils seront intégrés en début et en fin
Coupes d'Europe et des matchs de l'équipe de France
scène du logo de la marque) mais aussi durant les
matchs eux-mêmes (lors de mi-temps, durant les rappels
d'émission selon la technique du *billboard* (mise en
des scores ou les ralentis) et dans les bandes annonces[12].

Here the cues for reconstituting the text are quite different in type from in the sentence-jumbled version. Instead of dealing with semantic units we look for grammatical ones and instead of considering the functions we are searching mainly for forms. Whilst more difficult to complete, this exercise seems less useful for the insight it gives into the structure of text because it does not reward sufficiently the search for meaning beyond low-level grammatical units. Nevertheless both methods exploit the editing facilities of the software which enable the student by a few keystrokes to rearrange the text in the correct order and are clearly better done on screen than on paper.

Having up to now emphasized the discreteness between vocabulary-based and text-based exercises in the construction of word processed exercises it is, however, necessary to recognise that this distinction can and should be overcome. The link-up between the two resides in the functioning of nominal anaphora. The reading and writing of French can be enhanced by the recognition of the ways in which this mechanism functions in constructing text. In the following passage taken from *Le Monde* some of the examples of nominal anaphora have been removed and the role of the student is to restore the missing term or terms. As in previous exercises there are often various possible answers and the use of the synonym dictionary can again be a useful resource. However, by this stage the student should be more conscious of the relation between the choice of individual lexical items and the structure and functioning of text and should be making predictions according to textual and not simply lexical criteria:

> Trois mois après la signature d'une première lettre d'intention, IBM et Apple ont révélé mercredi dernier les détails de leur accord de coopération. Cette [1] historique réunit les deux [2], que tout opposait jusqu'à présent. Elle s'accompagne, pour chacun d'entre eux, d'un réaménagement en profondeur de sa stratégie et est extrêmement ambitieuse dans son contenu.

> Pour le président d'Apple l'[3] constitue "le fondement d'une renaissance". Pour le patron d'IBM c'est tout bonnement "la seconde décennie de l'ordinateur personnel" qui a pris corps. Le lyrisme employé est à la mesure du "big bang" que veut provoquer ce [4] spectaculaire. Deux mondes jusque-là totalement imperméables se connectent. Les [5] envisagées sont multiples: des microprocesseurs aux systèmes d'exploitation, des applications multimédias aux logiciels. Les possesseurs d'Apple ou d'IBM devraient ainsi pouvoir faire tourner indifféremment leurs programmes sur l'un ou l'autre [6], ce qui était impossible jusqu'à présent. D'ici à la fin de l'année, des solutions d'[7] devraient être proposées pour rapprocher les [8] existants. Cette [9] s'étend aux composants, les fameuses puces qui rendent intelligente une machine. Les deux [10] ont prévu d'équiper, à l'avenir, leurs [11] du même [12] dont la conception a été confiée à Motorola, le partenaire de toujours d'Apple, devenu récemment fournisseur d'IBM[13].

I have attempted so far to demonstrate how French word processing software can be used as a language-learning resource, showing how French expresses the concepts needed and how it is possible to produce a bank of easily updateable and expandable language exercises for students to practice. Without taking up the claim that word processing can render unnecessary dedicated CALL software[14], I hope to have established that it is a powerful instrument for creating exercises which are by nature variable in content and in level. I want, however, now to consider one way at least of embedding the use of word processing more closely in the course content instead of using it merely as a free medium for the creation of exercises.

Depending on the organisation of the degree programme it would be justifiable to introduce word processing in French at various points in a modular system, for example in a component on language varieties or on business technology. In the present case the students were following a combined studies programme which did not contain a business element and so it was essential for this course component to remain as general as possible and yet to be sufficiently focused so as not to seem an add-on or afterthought. The most natural entry-point for word processing in French seemed in these circumstances to be in an already existing second-year course component on French phonetics and orthography. The objective of this part of the course was to study the phonology and the articulatory phonetics of French and the structure of the orthographic system. The introduction of word processing into the course far from hindering these original objectives served to reinforce them.

From the beginning of the course, familiarisation with the management of the software and practice in phonetics can go hand in hand[15]. It is obviously unacceptable pedagogically to require students to copy-type passages of French in order to acquire or improve keyboard skills but it is quite appropriate to expect them to convert a phonetic transcription into standard orthography ("silent dictation") and to see the differences between the two systems of transcription. After overcoming the initial problems of recognition of the phonetic symbols for French it becomes clear to them that the system which poses the greater number of problems is precisely the one they have always practised. Another exercise which motivates the students to improve their keyboard skills[16] at the same time as moving between the written and spoken codes of French is the traditional exercise of dictation. Without advocating an obsessive cult of this exercise redolent of the French primary school system pre- or post-Chevènement, it is interesting to note that British students normally seem to react favourably to this ultra-conservative exercise which has for them, on the contrary, an almost exotic quality, particularly if done as pairwork.

Far from discouraging recourse to the spell-checking facilities during these types of exercises I wished the students to make full use of this extra resource but to be aware at the same time of its limitations. As we saw earlier, the nature of *Sprint*'s dictionary, which consists simply of a word-list containing actually occurring forms but does not take account of syntactic criteria such as agreement, is in itself a useful illustration of the multi-layered structure of the orthographic system. Similarly the problems with choices between homophones in the transition between spoken and written forms will not automatically be picked up and corrected. The software is to be perceived as a means of self-correction for a limited number of simple errors but more importantly as an aid towards understanding the nature of certain mistakes. It is not a mechanical panacea which imposes the correct answer but an interactive aid to learning. Moreover, the very shortcomings of the software can "humanise" the students' relations with the computer and can give them the incentive to fill in some of the lexical gaps in its knowledge by adding words to the dictionary.

Whatever the point at which word processing enters the curriculum in foreign language teaching its benefits should be both language specific and skills based. It is essential for it not to be viewed as an end in itself but as a teaching and learning tool for improving linguistic competence and as a starting point for developing experience and confidence in working with IT. From the analysis of student evaluation of the course component in question here, it emerged clearly that word processing had, in the students' opinion, increased their confidence in working with computers and added to the usefulness and enjoyment of the course. The follow-up to a formal introduction to word processing is obviously its regular use in the preparation and presentation of course assignments but also the transition to other types of software which can have CALL applications such as databases and hypertext.

Notes

1. For a useful listing and short description of CALL software available for different languages and at different levels see the current edition of the *ReCALL Software Guide* (Issue no.3, December 1992) produced by the CTI Centre for Modern Languages, University of Hull. The Centre also publishes a (free) journal, *ReCALL*, which contains reviews of CALL software and articles on the application of IT to language teaching in higher education. The other main journal in this field is *Computer Assisted Language Learning*, edited by Keith Cameron.

2. For examples of the "official" terminology of IT in French see the *arrêtés du 22 décembre 1981, du 30 décembre 1983, du 30 mars 1987, du 27 juin 1989*, published in the *Journal Officiel* and collected in the *Dictionnaire des termes officiels*, Délégation Générale de la Langue Française, 7th edition, 1991, pp.125-36.

3. Description of wardrobe taken from furniture catalogue.

4. Differences between French and German in the treatment of IT terminology originating in English are clearly brought out in a short article by J. Humbley in *Langue française - Langue anglaise. Contacts et conflits*, Strasbourg, 1986, pp.6-14, entitled "La traduction dans la terminologie de l'informatique de vulgarisation en français et en allemand". Humbley shows how French has less recourse to English loanwords than German in this particular area of technical vocabulary.

5. Such factors are taken into account in grammar- and style-checkers such as the French language version of Reference Software's *Grammatik* which reads word-processed files including those of *Sprint*. However, the new French language version of Microsoft's *Word for Windows 2.0* sets a new standard for word processing packages by including a built-in grammar-checker able to correct errors in *l'orthographe grammaticale*. For a discussion of the development of spell-checking and grammar-checking software in French see F. Marty, "Trois systèmes informatiques de transcription phonétique et graphémique", *Le Français Moderne*, vol.60, no.2 (1992), pp.179-97 and G.T. Yoka, "Le vérificateur d'orthographe: des analyses phonétique et lexicale à l'analyse syntaxique", *ibid.*, pp.198-208.

6. See her studies such as *L'Orthographe du français*, Nathan, 1980 and *L'Orthographe*, PUF, 1988.

7. This usage of the verb *décliner* is not given in the current (1987) edition of the Collins-Robert nor in the latest (1991) edition of the Harrap's *Shorter*. However, *New French Words* (Aberystwyth Word Lists) ed. G. Bremner, no date [1991?], gives an example of *se décliner* translated as "be adapted, undergo adaptation".

8. A typical example of such an authoring program is Eurocentres' *A Demi Mot*, a French-language version of Wida Software's *Gapmaster* or the multiple choice program *A Votre Avis (Choicemaster)*.

9. There are, of course, dedicated authoring programs which are designed for producing text reconstruction exercises. Two of the best known programs are Camsoft's *Fun with Texts* and *Eclipse 1.3*, the new version of *Storyboard*.

10. It is essential in this type of exercise for the text not to be longer than a full screen so that the whole passage can be viewed at the same time.

11. For a detailed study of the functioning of anaphora in French see F. Cornish, *Anaphoric Relations in English and French*, Croom Helm, 1986.

12. For this exercise the right-hand margin must be unjustified and each line marked with a hard carriage return in order to retain the line units when resequencing the text.

13. The terms used in the original passage are as follows: [1]alliance, [2]géants de l'informatique américaine, [3]accord, [4]rapprochement, [5]coopérations, [6]matériel, [7]interconnexion, [8]parcs, [9]mise en conformité, [10]firmes, [11]matériels, [12]microprocesseur.

14. This issue is raised in passing by I. Kemble and W. Brierley in "Computers and translation: integrating IT into undergraduate foreign language teaching", *Journal of Computer Assisted Learning*, (1991) 7, pp.170-7. For more ideas on the application of word processing to foreign language teaching see also the chapter by the same authors in their *Computers as a Tool in Language Teaching*, Ellis Horwood, 1991, pp.11-22.

15. A useful program for practising the phonetic transcription of French is *Apicale*, developed by and available from L. Wright at the University College of North Wales, Bangor. On the development of this program, originally produced for the BBC micro but now available in a PC version, see Wright's article entitled "APICALE: the Teaching of French Phonetic Transcription and Romance Philology" in *Use of Computers in the Teaching of Language and Languages*, ed. by G. Chesters and N. Gardner, Computers in Teaching Initiative Support Service, Bath, 1987, pp.107-113.

16. Students were given the choice between using the full AZERTY layout of the French keyboard available within DOS or generating the French characters via their ASCII codes. The great majority preferred the latter solution.

CALL and Video in the University Sector - the Bangor experience

Ben Fisher, University College of North Wales, Bangor

+ Laurie WRIGHT

It is undeniable that the students who are now coming into Higher Education have a very different profile from those of ten or even five years ago; GCSE, reformed A-levels and the advent of the UK National Curriculum have hastened the pace of change. There has certainly been a welcome improvement in the written and spoken fluency of the average student, but we can no longer assume that all incoming students have received any substantial formal training in grammar or translation into French, or that they will all have some knowledge of French literature. Thus there is a sense in which more traditional French departments in Higher Education have had the carpet pulled from under their feet, as it is no longer valid or productive to run courses which simply perpetuate the types of work students used to do at school, on the false assumption that these skills are still being taught there. We therefore need, in the broadest sense, new approaches, which include an introspective look at *what* we teach, *how* we teach it, and of course *why* we teach it. This chapter examines some answers, not necessarily complete ones, which have emerged within the University College of North Wales. There is no great master plan behind our developments; they are just current responses to the ongoing need for course development, trying to give students the best course we can. Inevitably, my viewpoint is that of an insider; I have been teaching in the French Department since 1987, at first part-time as a postgraduate, and latterly as a lecturer. Nevertheless, this perspective can, I hope, give more insight into the organic development of modernised courses than a bald statement of the techniques we use.

The first question, *what* we should teach, carries an extra point, i.e. who we are teaching it to? Today's students expect choice and we have to offer it if we are to attract the numbers we need to survive; as in most institutions, vigorous recruitment is needed just to maintain staff numbers. Our approach has involved the creation of a "French Language and Modern France" (a.k.a. "French B") degree running alongside "French" (a.k.a. "French A"). The two schemes offer different emphasis in language teaching, as French B offers enhanced use of communicative methods, authentic materials, and new technologies, particularly video and CALL, and a more linguistic/modern set of option courses - although there is a degree of cross-fertilisation between the courses, and they have a common first year. As may be expected in today's climate, French B is much the more popular, although there is a continuing demand for the more traditional course. Interestingly, the modern course also appeals to mature or otherwise "unconventional" entrants, who are an important factor for us as we have one of the UK's highest proportions of such students, typically 20% or higher across the College.

So what do we teach? Simply put, language plus a range of option courses from medieval poetry to contemporary cinema, taking in literature of most periods and types, art, social and political history, linguistic topics, current affairs[1], and commercial French. While this range embraces both degree schemes, any student can cover both ends of the spectrum; their choice of degree simply governs the predominant character of their options.

In other words, there is nothing strikingly original about the content of the UCNW courses. *How* we teach is the main perspective of this chapter. We have made a conscious effort to integrate new developments into the delivery of our courses, and to develop new courses to take advantage of the resources now at our disposal; although it should be added that some more traditional option courses, mainly literary, have stayed much as they were, and are no less popular for it.

The Role of Technology

It is widely recognised that authentic materials and new technologies are a "good thing" for language learning, but it often seems that an understanding of their rightful place in the curriculum is far from universal. It is easy to get excited about the current techno-fad - Satellite TV, CD-ROM, Interactive Video, or whatever - but much harder to integrate them into our teaching in a meaningful and productive manner. Enhancement of teachers' scheme of work is paramount, and curiously, the great flexibility we enjoy in the university sector is not always a benefit. Through Bangor's ESTEL Satellite TV research project[2] we have seen the need for school teachers to match new approaches to the strict parameters within which they work, primarily GCSE and the National Curriculum, and the Project's final recommendations have been made with a view to answering the needs of GCSE and the National Curriculum through relatively standardised applications of technology. In universities, parameters tend to be defined locally by departments, or even by individual members of staff who wish to work in a particular way. The result is great variety and pluralism in practice and methodologies; overall (and assuming the practice is good practice) this is, to my mind, one of the great strengths of UK universities. However, the relative shortage of external guidance or pressure means that there can be a certain hesitation and lack of direction when it comes to modifying the curriculum. This is exactly what can happen when we try to make the most of new approaches in modern languages.

CALL and Satellite TV for the First Year

Our first concerted attempt to modify teaching methods to integrate new approaches involved (logically) the first year, and language teaching in particular. We have used *Le Français en faculté* for the past five years and still find it an excellent resource, with a few slight reservations which have contributed to the way we expand on the book. For instance, the language class with 18-20 students meeting for two hours a week is not the best place to do the grammar/lexical exercises - for one thing, time is short, also less forthcoming students feel less need to come forward in class and may under-achieve as a result. Although GCSE and related developments have undoubtedly improved oral standards, getting (mildly stereotypical) shy first year students to take part in discussion is as difficult as it ever was. Enter CALL. We are fortunate that one member of the Department, Laurie Wright, is a talented programmer; he has developed his *Apicale/Lacuna* authoring systems (for BBC and more recently PC) very much with our Department's needs in mind. Using conveniently located computer rooms for classes, we have thus been able to create and exploit a bank of *Français en faculté*

CALL materials, including gap-filler versions of texts, corrected translations and *dossiers*, and computerised versions of the book's exercises, offering multiple acceptable answers, the ability to predict common errors, and a scoring system. Although CALL scores do not feature in assessment, the system can keep a coded record of each student's score. Part I students spend a minimum of an hour a week on CALL work, usually immediately after a class. Simple though the commands needed are, these sessions also of course enhance computer literacy; it is paradoxical that, however good microcomputer provision in schools and TVEI units may be, many of our intake still claim never to have touched a computer before arriving at Bangor. One is often led to conclude that computers in secondary education are often seen as a tool for low achievers, rather than as a means of support for all.

We also deviate slightly from the coursebook in use of Satellite Television, a resource we acquired at the same time as adopting *Le Français en faculté*. Mainly, it is used for discussion perhaps one week in four, replacing one of the less interesting or more dated texts, alternatively we often choose extracts which are relevant to current coursebook items - for instance work on TV adverts for the *Publicité* section, or political news to back up *La vie politique*. Satellite is able to provide material that avoids the dryness that can discourage students from learning a little about French political life; we recently found a slanging match (part genuine, part *Bébête Show* puppets) between Bernard Tapie and Jean-Marie Le Pen worked particularly well, both for raising awareness of public figures (in one group, all students knew about Le Pen while only one had heard of Tapie, and then only for his footballing connections) and expanding a type of vocabulary that the coursebook does not cover - *hé facho de mes deux!*, for instance. Typically we work with extracts three to five minutes long, with a worksheet including some vocabulary support and a transcription, sometimes with gaps in it. An extract of this length can easily provide an hour's class work (mainly vocabulary, aural/oral comprehension, *qu'est-ce que vous pensez de...* and so forth), and the soundtrack can then be adapted into a language laboratory exercise if desired. There is also, of course, the fact that Satellite Is Fun - or put more cynically, it dramatically reduces students' resistance to the learning process, just as it can in schools.

Authentic Material - How Authentic should we be?

Some teachers may ask, with genuine concern, "should we be teaching our students things like *hé facho de mes deux*? This is a problem with authentic material - where do we draw the line? Teachers at all levels often seem to choose "authentic" material suited to their own tastes: texts from *L'Express* or *Le Point*, video drawn purely from TV news or *L'Heure de Vérité*, for instance. This is all very well in itself and exposes students to very good French, but it does not prepare them for the much broader range of French they will have to cope with, for instance during their year abroad. It is not hard to find the written language we need to expand the range a little; any French newsstand provides a wealth of material, and there is no reason to confine departmental subscriptions to the more serious titles. *VSD*, for instance, offers a good compromise between hard news and populism, and it can be interesting, when seeking material for translation or discussion, to remember which is the most popular French daily paper. I am of course referring to *Ouest-France*, a very different product from the declining Paris *quotidiens*. And where are the C2's of French society, who do not appear on *L'Heure de Vérité*? They can be found as contestants on *Le Juste Prix* (*The Price is Right*), on *TF1* for the taking virtually every day of the week. Youth language? There is no shortage of it if we are prepared to consider programmes such as *Y'a pas d'lézard* on *M6* or *Salut tu vas bien?* on *Canal j*[3], although it is easy for staff to become figures of fun if they attempt to appear more *branché* than they really are. The language and culture of these groups are no less authentic for being less refined, and there is a high degree of appropriacy for our students, particularly those facing the year in France. I cannot have been the only twenty-one year old British student to have arrived as an *assistant* in a provincial *lycée technique d'état industriel* to find there was a type of French language nobody had taught me about, one that had to be absorbed fast in order to make the most of the year in France.

Authentic Video for the Second Year

Given these and other considerations, our second year language course for French B students now relies almost entirely on up-to-date authentic materials, with a heavy emphasis on video and audio work. In fact this approach evolved not so much as a deliberate policy as through our problems in finding a published course that suited us and our students. *Travaux pratiques* was used briefly some time back, and we also tried out *Lyon à la Une* as main resource for the second year. Although other institutions have developed very productive ways of using this course, it was not a great success for us. Some students commented that the modules reproduced work they had done at A-level, and it was hard to maintain interest in a single topic over two or three weeks; the variable quality of the video tapes, particularly their soundtracks, did not help. Overall we felt it was a course with a great deal of promise, much of which has been fulfilled with *En fin de compte* for the final year (a resource we are beginning to use), but which suffered from under-funding and a slightly too didactic approach to its use. We still use parts of *Lyon*, but only as isolated items. Batchelor and Offord's *Guide to Contemporary French Usage* is now used as a teaching textbook for the technical side of language, although class work concentrates on the sections on which students request or genuinely need coaching. Batchelor and Offord's emphasis on different registers of French is also well suited to a course in which satellite recordings are used as a source of contemporary French as spoken by a wide variety of speakers.

In place of *Lyon à la Une* we have developed a second-year course for French B which still relies heavily on video, meaning authentic video material drawn from satellite. The second year offers a good opportunity to expand students' French in a more relaxed manner than seems possible in the first and final years, and satellite is ideal for this as students do not always recognise it as a teaching tool, seeing the entertainment value first and foremost; resistance to learning melts away when small groups are asked to "sell" items to the class following the model of a teleshopping programme, or to create their own soundtracks for silenced TV adverts. The need for more serious assessed work is answered by work towards a written video comprehension test in the sessional exam, typically with three viewings of a two minute extract leading to a number of factual questions and a choice of longer *mettez-vous à la place de ...* or *écrivez une lettre à ...* questions. News is usually best for providing concise items containing facts and opinions, but other extracts (e.g. adverts, drama) can be just as effective. The exam also contains an aural test in which students write down a translation of a brief audio recording, and is completed by textual translations between French and English or Welsh.

Final Year Developments

As French B only reached final year level in the 1991-2 session, developments in that year are obviously fresh and may need fine tuning later on, although the first performances of students in degree examinations have been encouraging. The course builds upon second year video work with a more demanding written comprehension test, plus a more explicitly aural exercise in which students see a one-minute extract five times (once complete, three times edited into brief sections, once more complete) and prepare a transcription and translation of it into English or Welsh. Gist comprehension of difficult sections often means that the translations are slightly better than the transcriptions. This exercise is in fact a cousin of the traditional *dictée* (which we do not use), showing that "new" approaches need not always mean completely new departures.

Implications for Staff

Course developments of this kind inevitably have resource implications, in terms of staff and equipment. Creating a second degree scheme while leaving the existing one largely intact has brought with it increased demands on staff as regards time and flexibility. Apart from time spent on developing new course materials, teaching hours for most staff have not increased dramatically. Flexibility and shared hours between the two courses has ensured this, but often classes are larger than they might be, given the common problem of a worsening staff-student ratio. Staff adaptability has been just as important in a small department running two degrees with a very broad spectrum of option courses, as all staff make some contribution to both degree schemes. Staff have also had to get used to teaching courses quite distinct from their primary research areas. This does in fact have much to commend it in the current environment, as it can lead to pluridisciplinarity in research, and is (so to speak) an organic form of adaptation; just as French departments move away from teaching literature as the sole major discipline, staff can move towards combining literary research with work in other fields.

Language Labs for the Future

Equipment is of course a basic requirement for meaningful work with authentic video material and CALL. Modern Languages has long been viewed as a low-cost area in terms of equipment, but now that courses are becoming less paper/book-based, there is a good case for formal recognition of Modern Languages as a laboratory subject with commensurate weighting when equipment grants are being decided. We also need to consider how we can operate as a laboratory subject, and what sort of laboratory we wish to use. In other words, what is the future of the language laboratory?

The traditional tape-based language lab has as many drawbacks as advantages, and its use seems to be declining; for instance in our county (Gwynedd) there are now no operational labs in state secondary schools. Newer labs have many improvements, particularly regarding tape transport and indexing, but the basic weaknesses of tape technology remain; the physical demands of constant re-recording and winding push tape to and beyond its limits. Also, general performance can decline markedly as a lab gets older. In 1991 we found ourselves with two life-expired labs and finance to install one new one as a replacement. After much thought and evaluation of machinery, we chose to abandon tape altogether for our new lab, and in so doing we have, I feel, created an ideal workspace for new developments in the teaching of French and other languages.

As with our CALL work, the main credit for the initial conception (and most of the construction) of the new lab belongs to Laurie Wright. The lab uses voicecard technology; a voicecard is an add-on to a PC which allows it to emulate a tape recorder, making digital audio recordings on a hard disc drive. Unlike a tape recorder, there are no tapes to stretch and break, no heads to clean, and erasure is a simple matter of deleting a file - also the computer can only access the file it is instructed to, rendering echo from previous recordings impossible. With computer prices falling, a good entry-level PC now costs roughly the same as a language lab booth, so the old technology surely has limited appeal for the future[4]. Networking within the room is handled by a Tandberg TECS system (= *T*andberg *E*ducational *C*omputer *S*ystem), which is in fact intended for teaching computing to a class; the master console is linked to each booth by audio, providing the headphones we need, it can also monitor each student's display, and control student keyboards if required. A little extra wiring is needed to link TECS to the voicecards. Audio files are big - roughly 600KB per minute - and do not lend themselves to file compression, so only a few recordings can stay on each student's hard disc at a time; exercises are called up from a menu and copied by ethernet from a College fileserver; an added advantage of this is that each student can choose any one of several hundred exercises at any time. As this type of lab (apart from TECS) could not be bought off the shelf, we built it ourselves over the Summer 1991 vacation, adapting the furniture of one of the old tape-based labs to house computers securely.

The lab is not quite unique - we are aware of two similar ones in Germany, and ASC have recently installed a lab using both voicecards and tape recorders at

Aberystwyth - but we believe it is a leader in terms of its software and flexibility of use. The voicecards came with the *Voicedit* package, which is workable if relatively simple, and Tandberg also market a more sophisticated package called *Voicekart*. As with text-based CALL, we are using one of Laurie's programmes, *Oyez!*, which gives a visual representation of an audio recording as a series of lines over which a cursor moves; this eliminates the "guessing" involved in finding an exact spot on a tape recording, and teachers or students can insert markers isolating sections (as short as one syllable) which can then be repeated at will with complete accuracy. "Flagpoles" can be inserted, which prompt a student to record, or open a text window for (say) typing in a transcription or translation of an audio section. These answers can be scored. Alternatively, a running transcription (or vocabulary, or any other text) can be matched to the playback of the audio file. The lab can of course cater for purely text-based exercises too, and when we can afford the site licensing costs, it will offer networked CD-ROM dictionaries. Through the College network each booth can access the JANET network and beyond; we are currently working on Minitel access, with funding under the Enterprise in Higher Education programme. Video facilities are currently limited to a pair of VCR's and a large monitor, operated from the console, but in future each booth may be able to operate as an independent video workstation; the technology already exists to digitise short video extracts on a hard disc by means similar to the voicecard, and this can be incorporated at a later date when prices for video digitising cards drop. This type of lab has an added advantage in that although it has been relatively expensive to build from scratch (roughly £70,000 so far for twenty student positions, each able to accommodate up to three users), it should not need complete replacement at the end of its life as tape labs normally do. As components (computers, monitors, etc) expire or need upgrading, they can be replaced on a piecemeal basis, spreading the cost over a number of years.

There is considerable variety in the French materials available in the lab, depending on the courses involved. Of course, the CALL materials developed for the first year are on offer, along with audio recordings from other material (mainly video) included in the course. Materials also exist for second and final year language courses; the lab is a real boon for finalists, as they can practice for their video transcription/translation work with exercises that score their typed versions of audio material; this is an example of something that a traditional language lab simply cannot do. Option courses are also supported, and this is a developing field; some courses (e.g. more "linguistic" options) are suited to CALL materials analogous to those used with language classes, including audio work and (for instance) phonetic transcription. Other courses need something more akin to an information service, a need which is met by hypertext; we use the excellent (and simple) *Hyper* programme developed by Tony Elston at UWE (formerly Bristol Polytechnic), which allows users to move between pages of text using just four arrow keys. This type of service is used to house information on courses, their content (useful for those trying to choose which options to take next year), more general information (e.g. an introduction to word processing or a hypertext directory of library catalogues available on JANET), and in some cases work by the increasing number of students who word-process their assignments - particularly useful in a student-centred learning context. Where copyright allows, the lab's scanner (using proprietary optical character recognition software) can be used to computerise textual material for hypertext, removing the need to type.

At Bangor, virtually all Modern Languages teaching takes place in one building. In larger or more diverse institutions, digital technology allows a radical re-evaluation of the language lab as a facility. As our lab draws its software from a campus-wide computer network, *any* connected PC can access the material. Our students already use text-based exercises in other computer rooms, but the addition of a voicecard and headset could make any open-access PC in the College into a language lab booth, assuming that it has a hard disc drive. This offers the possibility of creating individual booths or small workgroups on any site connected via ethernet or a LAN of equivalent performance - for instance PC's on a science site could support non-specialist language learners, or machines in halls of residence could provide a convenient out-of-hours service. Although the use of TECS currently limits us to a twenty-position teaching lab, there is no theoretical limit to the number of PC's that could offer the same facilities for self-study. Many campuses have or are planning suitable networks (many existing first-generation ones are unlikely to be suitable), and the relatively low price of voicecards (roughly £200 apiece) offers a quick and inexpensive way towards flexible learning, using existing computing facilities.

Conclusion

I have left one question until the end: *why* we teach in the way we do. It is easy to go along with new developments simply because we are excited about the current "new toy", or because we may be resigned to what seems to be a new technological order imposed from on high. At the end of a day's in-service training I gave recently in a city area where all schools had cable television delivering foreign stations, I asked the group (rhetorically) whether they felt it was a good idea to make firm plans to use authentic video in their work; "do we have any choice ... ?", replied one teacher. The blunt answer is no, but we must be clear about our reasons and about implications for our teaching as a whole. This is particularly true in HE, where there is often a generation gap in departments; a recurring model is a department where most staff were recruited in the 1960's or early 1970's, and are only now being joined by a younger generation. There is a danger that new approaches can be seen as the private domain of younger staff, leaving their elders to carry on regardless until retirement. A balance is necessary, and we must not throw away the traditions of university French wholesale. Look, for instance, at the resurgence in interest in literature courses. We have observed that students who have not studied literature at A-level are often keen to begin it at university, whereas in past years many have opted to avoid it at all costs after suffering two years of indifferent French literature teaching in the Sixth Form. The changes in schools French teaching bring with them a new role for French in HE; we now provide (more or less by default) the stage where students learn the grammar they need to reach higher standards, where they are coached in translation, and where they may choose to immerse themselves in French literature. These are the things universities have always been rather good at; but of course we have to renew our work to some degree, simply because the lowest common denominator is lower than it was, particularly in terms of the grammar we can expect the average first year to have. Also, the emergence of the new universities in the UK requires that more traditional institutions take note of progressive work done in what is no longer a separate sector, while maintaining their cherished academic standards.

Given the work we have to do, it stands to reason that we must do it as efficiently as possible. Staff/student ratios get worse every year, and it is easy for teaching loads and administration to prevent lecturers fulfilling their contractual obligation to carry out research. New technologies can and do help. Satellite TV exposes students to a broader range of French than anything short of a trip to France can - a full range of speakers, accents and registers. It also motivates students far better than other media, and motivation is after all the first step to achievement. CALL, in its simplest text-based form, takes a lot of the drudgery out of language teaching, and although the novelty does wear off, students do respond well to it; a friendly "bleep" for getting an answer right can give as much satisfaction to an undergraduate struggling with the past anterior as to a four year old using *Fun School* on a home computer. In the more extended interpretation of CALL, involving combined audio and text, and ultimately video, we have a powerful tool which can perform tasks which are genuinely new, rather than just emulating what we have been able to do before. We are moving gradually towards truly useful multimedia; I am not referring to bought-in courses using laser discs, whose range will always be limited, but to multimedia we can create and adapt ourselves. Ideally this will involve digitised video mixed in with audio and text on a computer, but for the time being tape-based Interactive Video can be used to create exercises using authentic materials[5]. Such materials will of course be ideal for self-learning packages, either for students using a lab on a flexible basis, or working independently on a suitably equipped computer.

These tools are just that: they help us to do a job. They do not force us to rewrite every single parameter of our work, and they are not a threat. Of course, they offer us possibilities for new kinds of work, but this is nothing radically original, and no course can ever be considered "finished" from the development point of view. At Bangor, we have taken considerable steps towards meaningful integration of these new tools into our mainstream teaching, submitting them to the toughest of all evaluators: our students. The results are not always easy to quantify as there is no constant datum to measure them against - the student population changes in character almost every year, so it is hard to assess (for instance) what a student with little formal grammar has gained from CALL compared to a student taught conventionally who may have a better grammar background from schooldays. However, the overall impression leaves no room for doubt; students have opted *en masse* for the "modern" degree course, attendance and enthusiasm remain greater in video classes than in paper-based ones right up to Finals level (in other words long after the novelty value has gone), and we receive regular requests for computer enhancement for courses that as yet have little or none. We are fortunate, of course, in that our department contains the talent to write authoring programmes and that we have received funding for major research on Satellite TV in schools, with inevitable spin-offs for our own teaching; but the level of expertise and achievement that now exists in these fields around the country, along with the materials that are available, means that any institution can be confident that CALL and authentic video materials are a valid and above all productive part of the HE curriculum.

Notes

1. See my piece on the *La France au Jour le Jour* media-based current affairs course in the AFLS/CILT *French and the Enterprise Path* volume, London, 1992, pp.101-110.

2. ESTEL (Exploiting Satellite TElevision for Languages) was a two-year UCNW project funded by the Welsh Office (April 1990 to March 1992), working on the use of Satellite TV in schools in the context of central provision of multi-satellite systems to most Welsh secondary schools.

3. All these channels and more are available on the Télécom-2B satellite at 5 degrees West, in clear SECAM so a transcoder unit is needed to view them in colour on UK equipment.

4. For reference, the Bangor lab uses 386SX PC compatibles with 3MB of memory, 40MB hard discs and VGA colour displays. These have proved entirely adequate for our purposes, although a more powerful machine is used for creating materials.

5. The best IV system I have yet seen is the *Système Vidéo Assisté par Ordinateur (S.VAO)*, developed at Poitiers. It adds timecode to VHS tape, thus avoiding the notorious inability of VHS IV systems to find the right spot on the tape with sufficient accuracy.

Integrating New Technology: From Multimedia to Hypermedia

Chris Emery, University of Teesside

1. Introduction

Modern computer technology now makes it possible to integrate a huge range of multimedia teaching materials quickly and easily. At the touch of a button, it is possible to watch a video, listen to an audio recording, record and play back one's own voice, consult a dictionary or a grammar book, and call up information on linguistic functions or the cultural background of the language in question. Video compression, although still being developed, already makes it possible to do away with the video tape recorder or disk player and store moving video directly on a (large) hard disk. The cost of the equipment required is still high but no longer prohibitive and in any case is falling daily. Not surprisingly, there are many who regard multimedia CALL as a solution for the growing demand for language training and the shortage of trained language teachers.

This article will consider what impact the multimedia computer may have upon language teaching and discuss some of the difficulties which we are likely to encounter in the process of introducing it into the classroom. It draws heavily on the experience gained at the University of Teesside in the development of a multimedia introductory course in French, *France InterActive* which was started in 1990.

1.1. Traditional "Multimedia": Multimedia is not new

To get the issues into perspective, it is important to remember that the use of multimedia in language teaching is no longer a novelty. Since the 1970s, the use of multimedia has been a standard feature in language teaching in most institutions. There are few teachers who have not used a VTR or a television, an audio tape recorder, pictures and text in the course of a single lesson. The popularity of the BBC's television language courses, both in the home and the classroom is further evidence of the widespread belief that multimedia enhances the learning of foreign languages. Video and audio recordings are now used to emulate the native environment of the target language and confront the learner with authentic examples of the language itself. Books continue to pour off the printing presses and teachers continue to engage their students and pupils in interactive linguistic exchanges. There is nothing new about multimedia in language teaching.

However, this does not mean that multimedia CALL should just be slotted into existing teaching practices or will necessarily be welcomed by language teachers. In the first place, even a single multimedia computer is an expensive way to replace a television set, a video tape recorder and a pile of illustrated text books. If it is just to be used in a "traditional" way, one might as well stick to tried and trusted traditional equipment. Secondly, if a teacher wants to control the learning process and personally lead a class down a carefully constructed pedagogic path, a roomful of computers would probably be merely distracting and pointless. Introducing new technology into the classroom for its own sake will not necessarily improve either the teaching or the learning environment and we need to be aware of the reasons for this.

Three important areas on which we need to be clear are
1. the differences between traditional and computer-based multimedia;
2. the pitfalls of "hypermedia"; and
3. the impact on language teachers and teaching practices.

2. Computer-based Multimedia

Modern computer-based multimedia is nowadays often referred to as "hypermedia". It is a useful term, derived from the earlier "hypertext", and usually refers to libraries of multimedia materials which can be accessed in a non-linear, random fashion. The main advantages of hypermedia for learning are seen to be the near instantaneous access to a potentially unlimited range of materials and the control it gives the learner over the learning process. It would seem to be an ideal platform for the richness and variety of teaching materials used by language teachers. What then are the drawbacks?

2.1. Non-interactive?

Language is the primary vehicle of human interaction, and awareness of this underlies the modern tendency to emphasise the communicative aspects of language over the more traditional rule-based approach to language teaching. This shift in emphasis is to some extent being mirrored in the design of computer software in which "interaction", "virtual reality" and so on are the current buzz-words. However, language teachers have not been slow to point out the gulf that exists between human interaction and the "interaction" between man and machine. Today's computers, however sophisticated, are still deaf, unintelligent and non-empathetic and their "responses" are either pre-programmed by the author or controlled by the user. Any "interaction" with a computer tends to be largely one-sided or of brief duration.

But that is not to say that computers can not be extremely useful in stimulating reactions from the user. Reaction and response are intrinsic elements in human interaction and a great deal of language teaching initially consists in breaking down discourse into these elements. In particular, aural training and comprehension lend themselves to computerisation at almost any linguistic level. Spoken questions or instructions in the target language which require the learner to click on appropriate graphics or text or, for more advanced learners, a multiple choice quiz based on a news bulletin from TV5 require concentration and mental interaction with the subject matter.Text-based exercises (gap-fill, cloze, sentence reconstruction, grammar etc) compel the learner to read and write in the target language. At basic or intermediate levels the computer can be programmed to respond in turn to the learners input, providing feedback and correction. It is even possible to introduce simple role-play as has been done in France InterActive where the learner can take part in a video-based dialogue with the computer. Here the computer can not "assess" but only supply a model for the learner to imitate, but students thoroughly enjoy hearing themselves in conversation with a waiter, a *gendarme*, the doctor, etc. A computer does not have to be able to discuss the meaning of life to elicit a response from the user and interaction does not always have to be sophisticated to be useful.

2.2. Non-teaching?

Another contentious issue is the claim that computers can "teach". If teaching is defined as the transfer of "knowledge" (specific items of information which can be learned), then a case might be made for regarding computers as at least potential teachers. They can store vast quantities of information; they can present it, structure it, lead the learner step by step through pre-established paths from one item of information to another and often test whether this information has been absorbed by the learner. Moreover, unlike many human teachers, the computer has infinite patience.

Nevertheless, the question of teaching should be approached with some caution, since ultimately, if nothing is learned, surely nothing has been taught, however "good" the teacher may be. The determining factor therefore is not so much what is taught but how much is learned.

So it might be more helpful to concentrate on the *learning* process and for the moment regard teachers, computers or life in general as aids on which the learner can draw. This presupposes a learner-centred approach which is perhaps still rare in British education but which is inescapable if we are to release the full potential of computer-based learning. It also implies a degree of autonomy on the part of the learner which may be difficult to integrate into the established curriculum.

2.3. Teacher Control or Learner Autonomy?

The most effective learning is autonomous and not taught. As human beings we spend our entire waking lives learning and we do so effectively, usually effortlessly, in a continuous interaction with our social and physical environment. The process is autonomous in so far as it is initiated within ourselves by our own needs and is largely controlled by us. (Little, 1990) First language acquisition is a particularly powerful example of autonomous learning since it is clearly driven by the internal needs of the child and appears to be peculiarly resistant to external manipulation. Naturalistic second language acquisition may well follow a similar pattern even though there is some debate about the extent to which it is identical. But even if we accept Ellis's (1990) contention that implicit and explicit knowledge of the target language are separated in some way, there is little doubt that they are interconnected and that social autonomy and a spontaneous internal need to communicate are key factors in effective acquisition.

But in a formal learning environment where the initiative tends to come from an instructor such spontaneity and autonomy are necessarily reduced and sometimes even eliminated in the interests of discipline and curriculum requirements. Of course, good teachers try to bridge the gap between the subject matter and the actual needs of their pupils, thereby enabling them to turn "school knowledge" into "action knowledge" (Barnes, 1976) but it can be an up-hill struggle and results rarely reflect the input. If human teachers can not always bridge the gap, what chance has a mere computer which is relatively passive and subject to user/learner control?

In fact, what might be seen as a major weakness could prove to be its major strength. The introduction of the multimedia computer into the class-room provides an opportunity to rethink traditional teaching methods and replace expository teaching by a learner-centred approach which respects the autonomy of the learner. The passivity of the computer requires the learner to take the initiative but allows him to work at his own pace. So long as the subject matter is interesting and the linguistic level appropriate, hypermedia can open a window on virtual reality and stimulate exploratory learning. Our experience at Teesside has been that students find the interactive video (which was filmed in France) both fascinating and initially very difficult. The result is that they do a great deal of browsing between the different exercises (grammar, function, vocabulary) and the related video material. But there is a great sense of achievement when a dialogue in a noisy market has been thoroughly understood and they have heard themselves asking for a kilo of tomatoes and 100 grammes of "herbes de Provence". And having built their own "platform", they are also much happier to risk real interaction with the tutor!

3. Linguistic Input and Hypermedia

The *naturalistic* acquisition of language depends on linguistic input from the environment; and on the learner's need or desire to communicate. The input varies infinitely according to the learner's personal situation so problems of involvement and interest rarely arise. In the classroom the position is very different since the *need* to communicate in the target language is less urgent and naturalistic input is more limited. Teachers therefore have to provide learners with a wide range of input materials which will engage their interest sufficiently to activate those unconscious processes by which language is acquired naturalistically. (Little, 1990) To this end, textbooks, pictures, magazines and newspapers, audio tapes, film and television are brought to bear and some institutions have built up impressive libraries of multimedia language materials. The real challenge nowadays lies not so much in finding authentic language materials as in making them accessible to the learner in such a way that his autonomy is respected and his own interests fuel the learning process. This will not happen so long as the teacher always chooses the materials to be used and controls access to them.

Modern computer technology enables us to address that problem. The computer can be used to streamline and deliver the materials which a good teacher would use. It can free the teacher from the mechanical drudgery of switching machines on and off, opening books and writing on blackboards so as to concentrate on the actual language-teaching. It can be used to integrate the best features of traditional self-tuition so that even without a teacher, learners can choose from a wide range of authentic materials according to their own needs and interests on a self-access basis.

Finally, hypertext and hypermedia now give us a real choice between imposing linear paths of learning as in traditional CALL or adopting a model of discovery-based learning in which the autonomous learner explores the knowledge domain according to his own inner needs and interests. There is clearly a place for both learning styles, but if we are to exploit the flexibility that hypermedia offers, we must understand its nature and its limitations. In particular, we must be clear about the claim that it enables the computer to emulate the "real" world.

4. Hypermedia and the "Real World"

The range and flexibility of current hypermedia technology is certainly impressive but however sophisticated interactive hypermedia may become, it can not hope to emulate the reality of even the most mundane aspects of human existence. In the natural world the normal healthy human spends his or her entire waking life monitoring, filtering and interacting with information transmitted simultaneously via the five (some might claim six) senses. When we are communicating with others from a similar social environment, in our own language, verbal communication needs neither to be grammatical nor complete. (How often do people complete (or need to complete) their sentences?) We respond to gesture, tone, attitudes, even smell, and words are often no more than markers or pointers in a stream of multi-sense interaction. In fact, we often only really take notice of words when they are unexpected and require a reconstruction of what we have already anticipated. Our five senses together with a highly developed sense of "anticipation" surround us with "hypermedia" in its pure form and it would be fanciful to claim that present technology is in a position to emulate it.

Nevertheless, hypermedia does offer a powerful and flexible learning environment in which text, graphics, interactive video and animations; and interactive sound are combined. Furthermore, these features can be called upon simultaneously, autonomously and at random so that the user can have immediate access to any facility in any part of the system, each subset of which can possess its own interconnected nodes to be explored at will. The potential for enhancing learner autonomy is clear.

But there is also the danger of assuming that it is enough to provide the learner with the materials and then abandon him under the guise of encouraging autonomy and freedom. A hypersystem has no specific beginning or end and in the case of foreign language learning a complete "hyper" information base would have to contain a huge subset of the entire language and exploring it could be rather like being abandoned in a strange country without a guide book. One would doubtless survive but being plunged into an ocean of "authentic" language material may not always be the most efficient way of learning the language itself. Technological wizardry should not be used for its own sake nor should it be an excuse for the teacher to abdicate his responsibilities to the learner. It is one thing to encourage explorative learning and quite another to abandon the explorer altogether. If our explorer happens to be timid, unadventurous or just impatient his freedom to roam at will may result in his deciding to stay at home. It is not just in politics that "freedom" imposes the heaviest burden of all.

5. Signposting Hyperspace

5.1. The Interface

If learners are to take advantage of the autonomy offered by the computer, they need to acquire a cognitive framework, a mental map of the system before they can make effective use of it. Early trials of *France InterActive*, the hypermedia French course developed at the University of Teesside, revealed that this was the *only* thing that learners had in common. In attempting to construct their personal maps, no two individuals adopted an identical strategy. Some wandered around the system in an unstructured fashion, others tried rapid skimming, others browsed in a more relaxed fashion, some attempted to map things completely in advance while others just shouted for help. It became clear that the ability of users to keep track of where they were, where they had been and where they wanted to go, depended on a highly personal perception of the course. If they were not able quickly to build up a cognitive map both of the course and of the hypersystem underpinning it, interest diminished rapidly. In practice, just the provision of detailed navigational maps, even when not referred to, seemed to encourage browsing and enhance a sense of independence and confidence in the user.

Equally significant was the wide range of attitudes towards hypermedia and the learning process. Among our travellers in hyperspace there were at least three main types of learner: 1. Adventurers who just wanted to "see what happens"; 2. Explorers who liked to organise themselves but needed plenty of maps and guides; and 3. "Package tourists" who liked the adventure but wanted to be organised. They wanted to choose their tour and quit when they had had enough (interruption rather than interaction); but once embarked upon a lesson or a module, they expected to be told what to do and be carried along in an organised fashion without having to make constant decisions about "what to do next". Experience to date suggests that when it comes to computer-based training, there may be more package-tourists around than we might expect.

If we want to encourage learners to "learn" rather than sit passively and be "taught", we have to appreciate that the computer may initially constitute an additional barrier between them and the language-domain which they are to explore. Multiple windows which look like being the standard multimedia platform for the foreseeable future are by no means as "intuitive" as is claimed and for the inexperienced user the screen can rapidly appear cluttered and confusing. So the first step must be to ensure that the interface between the user and the computer is designed to encourage and facilitate the exercise of that responsibility. Human-Computer interfaces are varied and complex and there is a wealth of literature on their design and application. (Barker, 1989) It is hardly necessary to say that they must be friendly, comprehensible and uncluttered; they should encourage interaction between learner and computer and they must be appropriate to the function of each part of a lesson. (A video clip, for instance, needs a different screen from a vocabulary test or help on conjugation.).

5.2. Video and Windows

We found, in particular, that *France Interactive* placed heavy demands on the interface design because of the wide range of media involved (video, audio, graphics and text); the use of multiple windows and hypermedia; and the requirement of interactivity between the learner and the learning materials. These difficulties were further compounded by the combination of two contrasting environments: Video, effectively television, which users now rightly expect to be simple, direct and entertaining, and multiple Windows which, in spite of many virtues, can still appear highly complex and confusing to the inexperienced computer-user. If these environments are not carefully designed, they will dash the expectations of the user and create further barriers to user-autonomy.

At first sight, the facility to use multiple Windows seems to offer a powerful teaching environment. In *France Interactive* we have used it to create a model of the typical "desktop" of the modern language learner. Ideally on the desk there would be a television set for access to authentic material; there would be a tape recorder with record and play-back facilities; there would be a range of books (grammar book, dictionary, lesson books with exercises and tests); there would be writing materials and so on. All these features are available on screen at the click of a button; each has its own window which can be sized at will by the user; and all could be put on screen at once, though this would create an extremely untidy and confusing desktop.

The power of television to entertain, persuade and instruct is well-attested and the size of modern advertising budgets bears further witness to it. Early evaluation of *France Interactive* quickly established that half to full screen video attracted the most attention from users, whether or not they understood what was being said. This was due partly to the novelty of being drawn into a "virtual" France,and partly to the novelty of seeing "television" on a computer screen. But it was also a useful reminder that the modern computer-user has grown up with television and has acquired a degree of sophisticated televisual taste and expectations which multimedia producers must satisfy. This also extends to the quality of the graphics and cartoons. Furthermore, the power of television is rooted firmly in its relative simplicity and directness. In comparison with radio or books, it tends to *limit* the imagination but thereby focuses the attention more closely - but only if it is entertaining or interesting. It is all too easy to spend a great deal of money making ineffective video but it is not always easy to see why even high quality video is ineffective in teaching natural language. Effective use of a televisual medium puts a premium on designing the computer screen *and* the video materials so as not to cloud the clarity and immediacy of the visual message.

6. Language Teachers and the New Technology

Persuading language teachers to embrace the new technology is not always easy: as one might expect, attitudes among teachers range from enthusiasm to outright hostility. But the hostility is rarely generated by the technology itself. True, most language teachers are not intensive computer users and many regard the prospect of using the computer for anything more challenging than word-processing with some diffidence. But the most damage is done by a tendency among educational managers and fund-holders to regard the computer as an alternative to appointing new teachers or even to maintaining an existing establishment. The current emphasis on self-access and open learning and the pressure from government to increase student intake while holding down staff levels also encourage such attitudes. This is naive and very damaging. The new technology can help teachers (and learners) to make more efficient use of their time, but the only people able to introduce computers effectively into the classroom are the teachers themselves. To suggest that they will thereby make themselves redundant will ultimately prove self-defeating because if they do not embrace the new technology whole-heartedly it will not be used at all.

A major factor in this is that there are not (nor are there ever likely to be) any off-the-shelf packages which will serve everybody's purposes. Language is not like the workings of the water pump for which (in theory) a single piece of software might be used universally. The most likely direction to be taken by multimedia CALL is the creation of large libraries of materials (video, graphics, sound) from which teachers (as they do now) will make up their own courses. To do this, they themselves will need a clear understanding of what can realistically be achieved and a clear perception of how they want the software to function.This will require a commitment to and an understanding of the technology on the part of language teachers which will initially add substantially to their work load. Institutions will have to recognise this and budget accordingly.

This does raise some other more practical difficulties.

6.1. Practical Difficulties

To say that teachers must assemble the materials which they want for a class is to describe what they do already. To assemble them on a computer in such a way that learners can engage in some form of self-study is quite a different matter since it requires a level of computing skill which most language teachers will not possess. Current off-the-shelf presentation packages are linear and non-interactive and unsuitable for teaching. Language departments are therefore going to need programming support of some kind. The *France InterActive* team has tried to ease the problem for the Teesside Language Centre by offering a range of templates for different activities which only require the teacher to insert text and identify the video, graphics and sound required. But the templates for interactive audio and video are only semi-automated and require a programmer to complete the process.

Another serious problem is the cost of hardware. Multimedia computers are not cheap and the shortage of available software makes it difficult for small departments to justify a dedicated multimedia language laboratory. This is a vicious circle since teachers will not become involved in the development of teaching materials until there is a platform on which to mount them. The new University College in Stockton may be pointing the way forward by abandoning the idea of the dedicated language laboratory and installing multimedia computer laboratories which will be used where appropriate for any subject.

A final issue worth touching on is the number of organisational implications which introducing the new technology will have. Increased learner autonomy will not necessarily reduce the involvement of the teacher, but it will certainly change the *nature* of that involvement. As the computer takes over the more mechanical aspects of presenting materials and information and even the marking of basic grammar and vocabulary, so teachers can concentrate more on comprehension, communication and interaction. This will inevitably mean redesigning courses and timetables and rethinking the role of the language teacher in the classroom of tomorrow. It will be a challenging but exciting process.

7. Conclusion

The eventual introduction of computers and multimedia technology into the classroom is inevitable. But if it is imposed from above for reasons of economy or merely because it is fashionable, education will suffer. What we need to be doing already is defining the roles to be played in this new tripartite alliance and ensure that computers, teachers and learners bring to the partnership those things they each do best.

Interpreting from a video source: teaching and evaluation

Phil Powrie, University of Newcastle upon Tyne

From being the preserve of universities such as Bradford and Salford, interpreting is now increasingly incorporated into French undergraduate degrees in universities, either as a specialist option, or as an obligatory part of the core language course. A survey undertaken in June-July 1991 showed that at least 22 higher education institutions now teach interpreting in the UK, of which about half are not those ex-polytechnics or universities which traditionally have a specialist bias towards intensive language skills[1].

"Interpreting" needs to be more closely defined, since it covers variable practices. The survey showed that the form of interpreting most used is liaison, defined as interpreting a dialogue between an English speaker speaking in English and a French speaker speaking in French, either from a scripted source or from spontaneous discourse (20 instances). This is followed by consecutive interpreting, defined as waiting until the speaker has completed the discourse, or a section of the discourse before interpreting it (10 instances). Simultaneous interpreting is taught less frequently still (6 instances), mostly by universities which tend to be associated with technical skills of this type (Bath, Heriot-Watt, Salford). Three institutions teach all three modes, and nine teach at least two modes.

It is not my intention in this paper to go over ground which has already been covered by Bradford's excellent collection "Interpreting in the undergraduate course" (see Griffiths, 1984, Henderson, 1984, Pollock, 1984). I shall concentrate on two issues not covered in that collection: the use of authentic video material and problems of evaluation in an interpreting course. The comments I shall make are based on experience of designing and teaching an interpreting/summary course in the Department of French Studies at the University of Newcastle upon Tyne since 1988.

Aims and History of the Course

The aims of the course are inextricably bound up with its development. The interpreting element was originally conceived as one of several listening skills for all students in the final year (transcription, summary, interpreting), to which one weekly hour was devoted, building upon what had originally been a purely oral summary course in the second year. Very quickly, however, students made it clear that they wanted more time devoted to the interpreting element, to which only five classes in the final year had been given over. The reason for this was that they recognised it as a marketable skill, and quite correctly felt that they would be unlikely to improve if only a handful of classes were devoted to it. This led to the creation of a separate weekly interpreting hour in the final year, and the combination of interpreting and oral summary in the second year. With such an emphasis, the aims of the course changed. From being a complement to other listening skills, the course was redesigned to incorporate the following aims:

- To improve the communicative competence of the students by developing a capacity for rapid response, clear articulation, fluency, and lateral thinking, in addition to the accuracy required of any form of translation. If our students are to become the type of articulate communicators supposedly required by employers, the laborious and usually solitary meticulousness of written translation skills will only partially develop that competence.   This led to the decision to use dialogue as well as monologue for interpreting, since a reasonably authentic informal situation of the type mentioned might well involve several speakers. Our primary aim, therefore, was not to provide specific vocational training, since most of our students will never become professional interpreters, although some may well be called upon to act informally as interpreters in the course of their employment[2].

- To prepare our second-year students for their year abroad by sensitising them to French speakers speaking in authentic situations.

Combination of oral summary and interpreting proved awkward in the short term, since students often blurred the distinction between the two in practice. The combination was useful in the long term, however, precisely because it allowed formal distinctions to be made between the very different operations involved. Indeed, in a few cases, the two exercises are based on the same videotext (this is the case in the example given in the Appendix) so as to train students in the different approaches required.

From its inception, the course followed very closely the pattern established by Brian Griffiths in Bradford (Griffiths, 1984), i.e. practice on increasingly longer items without note-taking at the beginning of year 2, moving on to note-taking practice on short items, and again gradually building up to more extended extracts, whether for summary or for interpreting.

The standard summary exercise practised mainly in second year involves viewing an extract of continuous monologue or occasionally dialogue, twice. Students then prepare a summary either in French or more often in English using their notes, and are required to deliver the summary within a specific time limit, anything between 45 seconds to 2 minutes depending on the length of the extract and its complexity. The time-limit is made clear to them before the first viewing. The reason for the time-limit is that students often failed to discriminate between important and less important points, and in extreme cases were close to interpreting the piece. Initial use of the timed exercises at the beginning of the course leads to garbled summaries, but students soon understand how to judge the time available to them, and perform better as a result.

The standard interpreting exercise practised throughout the two years and examined at the end of the final year is consecutive interpreting (as defined above) of a discourse on videotape lasting 3-10 minutes which the students view once in its entirety, and a second time paused into several fragments, each fragment being interpreted by the students and recorded for evaluation. Considerable variation occurs in class over the two years, however: liaison interpreting (either with the tutor reading and/or improvising a dialogue in French and English, or a live improvised dialogue with a native speaker) and consecutive interpreting with only one unpaused hearing are also used.

The material used is nearly all taken from the language package *Lyon à la Une*, and could be described as general rather than technical. This is described in the following section.

The Use of Video Material

Unlike audio material, video allows you to watch the speaker. This is self-evident, of course. Its importance cannot be underestimated, however. Unlike the professional interpreter, who more often than not works in complete isolation in a booth, usually listening, but not watching a speaker, the type of situation which underlies this course (interpreting in an informal context) would clearly involve the presence of all the speakers concerned. Gesture in this context becomes all-important as a communicative code, often resolving otherwise intractable problems of meaning. In the case of second-year students, it allows them to analyse gestural codes in authentic situations which will help attune them to Gallic specificities and make them feel less estranged in their year abroad. Students are therefore encouraged to watch the speaker or speakers carefully, and to take only miminal notes on first screening, the brief being to understand the shape and the detail of the communication as fully as possible. They then rarely watch the whole of the second, paused screening before giving their version of the discourse, since ideally the bulk of their note-taking occurs during the second screening.

Given the parti pris of non-technical authentic situations for this course, the choice of video material was not just pedagogically appropriate, but a practical choice, since a number of video packages exist (*En fin de compte*, *Itinéraires*, *Lyon à la Une*, *Une Vie d'Etudiant*), as well as the possibility of recording items from TV5. In practice, we have found that *Lyon à la Une* is the most convenient source for a number of reasons:

- Unlike *En fin de compte*, it contains extensive transcriptions, which are an absolute prerequisite for designing a course based on paused extracts if the teacher is not to spend considerable time preparing transcriptions.

- The material is organised into extensive modules, thus allowing in-depth exploration of particular issues (racism, the world of work), and their specific lexis.

- Although the material is constrained by the interview situation, it has ordinary people talking in spontaneous French(es), whereas much of the material on *Une Vie d'Etudiant* is scripted and occasionally stilted. Although we do use TV5 news material later in the course (and for the examination) when the students are more proficient, it has the disadvantage of tending towards restricted varieties of French (newscaster/reporter French; formal interview French). There are further disadvantages with the systematic use of TV5 news items:

> - they are usually carefully crafted linguistically, and therefore too dense;
> - the delivery is too rapid;
> - they are too short (an average of 1 minute 30 seconds) to be of any practical use for sustained interpreting unless they are presented as compilations.

Of more use are the extended interviews of *Sept sur Sept*, which at least sometimes avoid the problems mentioned.

Although much of the video material of *Lyon à la Une* was never intended to serve as an interpreting source, it has proved remarkably successful. The material has been systematically exploited as follows, with very little of each module being omitted:

Year 2

Wks 1-4   Short-medium-long live-source items for memory work. Introduction to note-taking.

5-9   Module "Détente" on specific leisure activities in and around Lyon (swimming, cinema); ending with attempts to interpret jokes told by children.

10-18   Module "Les banlieues chaudes" on racism in Lyon.

19-22   Module "Radio Scoop" on a local radio.

Year 3

Wks 1-9   Module "Le monde du travail" (work meeting at the *Galeries Lafayette*; interviews with job-seekers; trade-union meeting).

10-13   Module "La Une contre la montre" on the *Dauphiné Libéré*.

14-15   Module "Chez Rose" on wine-making.

16-18   Module "Chiens écrasés" on *fait divers*.

19-22   Previous exam pieces, usually taken from TV5.

The *Lyon à la Une* video material is sufficiently varied in subject, speaker, register, speed, etc., for a two-year interpreting/summary syllabus to be devised. As can be seen, some modules seem more appropriate for specific years. Thus, in the year prior to their year abroad, it is useful for students to become aware of some of the difficulties faced by Lyon (the module on racism), given that most of them will find themselves in major cities. The modules chosen for use in the final year deal more with the world of work, as is appropriate to finalists; and more importantly, the monologues/dialogues are denser. Some modules, or parts of modules lend themselves to the encouragement of a lighter mood, such as the module on wine and food, or the attempts to interpret jokes told by children at the end of the module "Détente".

Evaluation of Performance

It was originally decided that staff would not mark recorded cassettes each week, since this would be too onerous in addition to other exercises in the core language course which required evaluation. It was simpler, it was felt, for students to listen to each other's recorded performance, either in class or outside class, and to comment on it, with the tutor listening in on as many as possible.

Student reaction to this type of evaluation was not positive. Despite considerable guidance as to what was expected in individual exercises, students felt that they were insufficiently monitored, one of the major problems being the lack of consistency, inevitable with a multiplicity of individual student assessors. This led to a range of possible solutions, each of which has been tried:

1. Distribution of an original transcript.
2. Distribution of a marksheet with a summary of points in French.
3. Distribution of a marksheet with a summary of points in English.
4. Distribution of a marksheet with the whole of the discourse translated in separate points in English together with qualitative criteria.

Distribution of an original transcript was by far the easiest solution in the case of *Lyon à la Une*, since these existed as part of the package; it was certainly an easier option than the labour-intensive distribution of a translated transcript. The problem with it was that students could not easily follow both a French script and the translated variant of it recorded by their colleague, as well as retaining sufficient distance for a critical appraisal. Moreover, the critical appraisals were very variable, and often too impressionistic to be of much value.

It was clear, therefore, that a more automatic system had to be found.

Distribution of a marksheet with a summary of points in French which gave the gist of the piece, although easier to handle, was less useful still, since not only was there the problem of a second level of translation, there was in addition the need to extrapolate from the summary to the fine detail. This was only partially resolved by the third solution of distribution of a marksheet with a summary of points in English, where the problem of extrapolation remained. In the case of both of these approaches, a markscale was introduced, which tied the number of points to the departmental marking scale; this aspect was retained for the last solution.

The last solution was to translate the whole piece, not just its keypoints, and to make it more user-friendly by separating it into numbered points which the appraiser could simply tick. In addition, it was felt that account should be taken not just of the content of the piece, but of the ability of the interpreter to communicate that content fluently, clearly, and so on. After a few trial runs, the system currently used is shown in the appendix, which contains a transcript of a piece from *Lyon à la Une*, with two exercises based upon it: a summary, to be done within a specific time-limit as mentioned above; and an interpreting exercise (the breaks in the script indicate pauses for the interpreting exercise). In both cases, the mark-scale is based on the one currently used in the department, five points within each of six bands going from 21-79. The tutor collects student marks after each exercise.

Three qualitative criteria are taken into account:

- Fluency: lack of hesitation and repetition; success in overcoming linguistic gaps in the original discourse, i.e. providing the appropriate "filler" so that the interpretation is fluent.

- Grammatical competence: command of English sentence grammar and lexis; avoidance of gallicism, i.e. literal translation where this would not be appropriate English.

- Expressive competence: clear pronunciation (i.e. clarity of articulation), and intonation (i.e. avoidance of monotone).

Each of these criteria is assessed on a short scale of 0-5 corresponding to degree classes, and may affect the position achieved on the content scale. We decided, however, not to allow the qualitative criteria to affect the class achieved by accuracy of translation. Our view was that such accuracy, i.e. clear understanding and interpreting of the message, is considerably more important than the qualitative or performance skills criteria. The decision also takes into account the tendency of the students to be overly generous in their assessment of what, say, first-class fluency might mean.

One disadvantage of this form of evaluation is that the presentation of a single written translation tempts the students to see interpreting as an oral version of written translation. Considerable work must therefore be done to explain how the translated text should be used merely as a guide for evaluation, and this necessarily needs to be followed by pair and class discussion of alternative renderings, as well as discussion of what makes oral production distinctive (the "qualitative criteria" mentioned above). This disadvantage is a small price to pay, in our estimation, given the advantages of using student evaluation with marksheets.

A second disadvantage is peer evaluation. The ideal evaluation is by the course tutor, who could on a regular basis collect the recordings and evaluate them. Although pedagogically desirable, this is simply too time-consuming to be done on a weekly basis[3], and is reserved for strategic points during the course. The disadvantage can, however, be turned into the first of several advantages.

The first advantage is that students feel that they are being closely monitored both by their peers, and by the tutor. This encourages a certain level of concentration, as well as generating sometimes heated post-exercise discussion, focusing on the appropriateness of the summary points selected, for example, as well as specific issues of translation.

The second advantage is the possibility of establishing a norm. The correspondence of the points scale to the mark scale is established empirically over two or three years, in the sense that it is quite possible that a piece will yield either extremely high or extremely low marks. Adjustments need to be made according to what is felt to be the general level of attainment of a particular year-group. An interpreting norm for specific material can then be established, which allows closer monitoring and guidance.

A third advantage is that it helps students focus on the detail of what we require of them. Our experience is that this reassures them, both because they can see how they might be improving during the course of the year in simple numerical terms (they invariably do), and because they know that the same system will be used in the examination.

To conclude, I would like to discuss briefly a further modification which we have recently introduced experimentally: to ascribe more points to what might be considered the keypoints of an extract. Students have been quick to point out how separating a text into a number of points with equal value could in theory lead to distortions. As is always the case, the course will improve as we take account of student judgements, just as we hope that they will improve their accuracy of translation and communicative performance skills as a result of our judgements.

References

Brian Griffiths (1984), "The ear has its reasons - interpreting and the modern languages curriculum", *Bradford Occasional Papers: Essays in Language, Literature and Area Studies*, 5 (Spring 1984), pp.113-40.

John Henderson (1984), "Language performance, context and the personality of the interpreter", *ibid.*, pp. 141-54.

Michael T. Newton (1992), "Survey of Career Destinations, Skills Development and Language Usage: Graduates of the B.A.(Honours) Degree in Modern Languages at the University of Northumbria (formerly Newcastle Polytechnic) 1975-1990" (September 1992).

Richard Pollock (1984), "Towards a pedagogic theory of interpreting: learning to interpret, or interpreting to learn ?", *Bradford Occasional Papers: Essays in Language, Literature and Area Studies*, 5 (Spring 1984), pp.92-112.

Barbara Phillips-Kerr (1991), "Survey of Career Destinations: 1985 Modern Language Graduates of the Universities of Bradford, Hull, Newcastle upon Tyne, Sheffield and The Polytechnic of Newcastle upon Tyne", University of Newcastle upon Tyne Careers Advisory Service Publication, May 1991.

Phil Powrie (1992), "Interpreting in the undergraduate French degree: a national survey 1990-1991", *Francophonie*, 4 (June 1992), pp.18-22.

Notes

1. A questionnaire was sent to all 53 universities and 29 polytechnics in the UK which currently teach undergraduate French degrees (London and Wales colleges were treated as separate institutions). 45 institutions out of a possible total of 82 responded (return rate of 54.9%). The following 22 institutions taught interpreting in 1990-91 (26.8% of the total of 82, although of course some institutions which did not respond are known to teach interpreting). These institutions are designated by their current names: the universities of Aberdeen, Aberystwyth, Aston, Bath, Central Lancashire, Greenwich, Heriot-Watt, Kent, Leeds, Leeds Metropolitan (Leeds Business School), Liverpool, Newcastle upon Tyne, Northumbria, Portsmouth, Reading, Salford, Sheffield, Sheffield Hallam, Westminster, West of England at Bristol, plus two universities which preferred not to be named. See Powrie (1992).

2. Of 177 students graduating in modern languages in 1985 in the universities of Bradford, Hull, Newcastle upon Tyne, Sheffield and the then polytechnic of Newcastle upon Tyne, not a single one was employed as a professional interpreter in 1991, although one had a further qualification as a Royal Navy Interpreter in Swedish; only three were employed as translators; see Barbara Phillips-Kerr (1991), pp.4, 6. A similar survey covering only the modern languages graduates of Newcastle upon Tyne Polytechnic 1975-1990 gives a similar result: not a single interpreter, three employed as translators, and one further qualification of translator/interpreter (Spain). Interestingly, of the 55 graduates for whom the use of languages was a key factor in gaining their first employment, interpreting came joint fourth with reading reports/journals (50 instances) after using the telephone (80), talking to colleagues or clients (77), writing correspondence (62), with translation running a poor sixth (38) (Newton, 1992, 22). Students are not only required to act as informal interpreters in future employment of course; this may well happen in their intercalary year, as Irene Wells, Head of the Division of Languages at The University of Greenwich pointed out in response to my questionnaire.

3. As is confirmed by my survey. The preference where monitoring during the year is concerned is clearly for informal evaluation by the tutor in the class situation (20 out of 22 institutions), backed up by occasional formal evaluation of a recorded interpretation outside of class time (16), so that 4 institutions never use recorded student production for evaluation during the course of the year. Group evaluation is in comparison little used, with only 9 instances of informal evaluation by the group in a class situation, and a very small number of instances of formal evaluation by the group using marksheets (5). See Powrie, 1992.

Appendix

Paused transcript of the "Archevêque de Lyon", *Lyon à la Une*, Module 2, "Les Banlieues chaudes", pp.2.35-2.36

D'autre part, mais ceci est, je crois, également propre à d'autres pays (peut-être qu'en France nous le sentons davantage) il y a le problème de l'immigration, plus précisément, la manière dont l'ensemble de la population française se comporte par rapport aux immigrés. // Quand il s'agit des immigrés euh très proches de nous...latins, si vous voulez, portugais, espagnols, italiens, les choses se passent encore assez bien. L'intégration dans le respect de l'identité, oui, se passe, je crois pouvoir le dire, assez bien. Si vous interrogiez les Italiens, les Espagnols et les Portugais, vous auriez vraisemblablement une réponse asses positive dans bien des cas sur la manière dont ils sont accueillis, // du moins avant que le problème du chômage ne rende un peu plus aigüe la question de cette cohabitation. On les accuse quelquefois de prendre le travail des Français, ça, c'est un problème nouveau depuis la crise que vous connaissez. Par contre, il est devenu plus difficile pour l'ensemble de la population d'accueillir les les Maghrébins, les gens d'Afrique du nord...surtout Algériens, Marocains, Tunisiens. // Quelquefois même cela devient une attitude d'intolérance, avec un engrenage. Il y a une situation d'engrenage, pourquoi ? Parce que la population ressent confusément, à tort ou à raison, que les Maghrébins concurrencent le le travail, sont source de chômage. Pour ma part, je ne le crois pas mais, tout de même, c'est le sentiment général. D'autre part, les Maghrébins se sentent rejetés, en tous cas moins accueillis. Le type de logement qu'on a fait pour eux ne contribue pas à l'intégration. // Je ne sais pas comment rompre ce cercle qui devient un cercle de la violence dans certains quartiers de Lyon, en tous cas de la banlieue de Lyon. C'est l'un des grands problèmes que nous rencontrons aujourd'hui. Et dans le quartier dit des Minguettes, la ZUP des Minguettes de Vénissieux, il est devenu dramatique. Tout récemment un policier a été blessé et un jeune Maghrébin était blessé. Dans la nuit d'avant-hier, deux policiers ont été légèrement blessés également, des commerçants ont commencé la grève de la faim, hier soir, j'ai moi-même publié une déclaration, qui paraît aujourd'hui même dans la presse, dans laquelle je fais appel à à la paix sociale. // Il se fait que les jeunes Maghrébins, qui ont engagé une grève de la faim il y a deux mois, m'ont demandé ma médiation. J'ai cru devoir répondre, tout en prenant une certaine distance, à leur appel, c'est la raison pour laquelle j'ai ressenti peut-être plus que d'autres le drame de cette immigration et notamment de la situation actuelle des Maghrébins. C'est un problème urbain, particulier aux grandes villes, pas particulier à Lyon.

NAME OF CANDIDATE.....................

Archevêque de Lyon: interprétation

Each numbered statement represents a point. Listen carefully to your partner's production (you may well need to listen two or three times in places) and give your partner
* a whole mark if the sense of the statement is carried;
* a half-mark if the sense is obscured by poor English;
* no mark if no attempt is made to translate the material;
* half-mark if there is a misunderstanding.

Add up the marks, and place them on the scale opposite by ringing an appropriate number, or inserting the number if it does not correspond exactly to the marks on the scale. Then discuss your partner's production with her/him, being prepared to justify your marks.

1. On the other hand,
2. but this is equally true of other countries
3. (perhaps we feel it particularly strongly in France)
4. there is the problem of immigration,
5. or more precisely,
6. the way in which the French population as a whole
7. behaves towards the immigrants.
8. When it is immigrants who are close to us
9. the Latins if you like,
10. Portuguese,
11. Spanish,
12. Italians,
13. things are not too bad.
14. Integration does not pose too many problems.
15. If you were to ask the Italians,
16. the Spanish,
17. and the Portuguese,
18. you would probably
19. get a fairly positive response in many cases
20. concerning the way in which they have been accepted [half for "welcomed"]
21. at least
22. until the problem of unemployment
23. sharpened cohabitation as an issue.
24. They are sometimes
25. accused
26. of taking work from the French;
27. this is a new problem
28. since the beginning of the crisis.
29. On the other hand,
30. it has become more difficult
31. for the majority of the population
32. to accept the North Africans [no mark for "Magrebins"]

33. especially the Algerians,
34. the Morrocans,
35. and the Tunisians.
36. Sometimes
37. this turns into intolerance,
38. a vicious circle.
39. Why ?
40. Because the population feels,
41. rightly or wrongly,
42. that the North Africans are competing for jobs,
43. are a source of unemployment.
44. For my part,
45. I don't believe it,
46. but it is the general feeling.
47. Then again [accept "on the other hand"]
48. the North Africans feel rejected,
49. at any rate less well accepted.
50. The type of housing [no mark for "lodging"]
51. built for them
52. does not help integration.
53. I do not know how to break this vicious circle,
54. which has become violent
55. in certain areas of Lyon,
56. at least in the suburbs of Lyon.
57. It is one of todays's great problems.
58. And in the area of Les Minguettes,
59. the ZUP des Minguettes in Vénissieux,
60. it has become dramatic/things have taken a dramatic turn.
61. Just recently
62. a policeman was injured [accept "wounded"]
63. and a young North African too.
64. During the night
65. the day before yesterday,
66. two policemen were also slightly injured,
67. some shopkeepers
68. began a hunger-strike,
69. yesterday evening [do not accept "last night"]
70. I published a declaration,
71. which will appear in today's newspapers,
72. in which I appealed for peace [half only for "social peace"].
73. It so happens that the young North Africans,
74. who started a hunger-strike
75. 2 months ago,
76. asked me to mediate.
77. They asked me because they consider me to be a man of God
78. and a friend.

79. I felt I had to respond to their appeal,
80. although keeping a certain distance.
81. That is perhaps the reason why
82. I have felt more acutely than others
83. the drama of immigration,
84. and especially the present situation of the North Africans.
85. It is an urban problem,
86. which occurs in all large cities;
87. it is not peculiar to Lyon.

Points	Mark
87/86/85	79
84/83/82	77
81/80/79	75
78/77/76	73
75/74/73	71
72/71/70	69
69/68/67	67
66/65/64	65
63/62/61	63
60/59/58/57	61
56/55/54/53	59
52/51/50/49	57
48/47/46/45	55
44/43/42/41	53
40/39/38/37	51
36/35/34	49
33/32/31	47
30/29/28	45
27/26/25	43
24/23/21	41
20/19	39
18/17	37
16/15	35
14/13	33
12/11	31
10/9	29
8/7	27
6/5	25
4/3	23
2/1	21

NAME OF CANDIDATE.....................

Archevêque de Lyon: précis (1 min 30 secs maximum)

Each numbered statement represents a point. Listen carefully to your partner's production (you may well need to listen two or three times in places) and give your partner
* a whole mark if the sense of the statement is carried;
* a half-mark if the sense is obscured by poor English;
* no mark if no attempt is made to translate the material;
* half-mark if there is a misunderstanding.
Add up the marks, and place them on the scale opposite by ringing an appropriate number, or inserting the number if it does not correspond exactly to the marks on the scale. Then discuss your partner's production with her/him, being prepared to justify your marks.

1. Immigration is a problem for many countries.
2. In the case of France, it is less of a problem for immigrants who are close to the French,
3. such as those from the Latin countries.
4. These are reasonably well integrated.
5. Except that some people accuse them of causing unemployment for the French.
6. There is on the other hand quite a lot of intolerance of North Africans
7. People accuse them of causing unemployment.
8. They feel rejected.
9. This can escalate into violence
10. as has happened recently.
11. A policeman and a young North African were injured
12. in the Minguettes district of Lyon.
13. And the day before yesterday
14. two more policemen were injured,
15. shopkeepers began a hunger strike.
16. After some young North Africans asked for my help,
17. I broadcast an appeal yesterday evening
18. calling for calm.

Points	Mark	Points	Mark	Points	Mark
18	79	17	75	16	71
15	69	14	67	13	65
12	63	11	61	10	59
9	57	8	55	7	53
6	51	5	49	4	41
3	39	2	31	1	21

Qualitative criteria (used for both the summary and the interpreting exercises)

- **Fluency** (lack of hesitation and repetition; success in overcoming linguistic gaps in the original discourse, i.e. providing the appropriate "filler" so that the interpretation is fluent.

Ring: 0   1   2   3   4   5
        Fail   Non-Hons   Third   Lower Second   Upper Second   First

- **Grammatical competence** (command of English sentence grammar and lexis; avoidance of gallicism, i.e. literal translation where this would not be appropriate English)

Ring: 0   1   2   3   4   5
        Fail   Non-Hons   Third   Lower Second   Upper Second   First

- **Expressive competence** (clear pronunciation and intonation)

Ring: 0   1   2   3   4   5
        Fail   Non-Hons   Third   Lower Second   Upper Second   First

Now add up the three qualitative criteria marks to give a mark out of 15. On no account should the qualitative mark change the degree class established by the content mark.

A mark of 0-4 scales down the mark within the class given in the content scale, by however many points are available to correspond to the number of points to be scaled down.

A mark of 5-10 does not change the content mark.

A mark of 11-15 scales up the mark within the class given in the content scale, by however many points are available to correspond to the number of points to be scaled up.

TOTAL:

Integrating Authentic Material and New Approaches in the Teaching of Engineers

Michèle Dickson, University of Strathclyde

Started five years ago, the "French for Erasmus Students" courses at Strathclyde University now count 440 students. This paper presents our attempts over the years to deal with the problem of relevant material by defining our priorities, reflecting on what type of material to choose in the light of various lines of research in linguistics, how to use the material to by-pass the narrow confines of specific needs, and the change towards a more cognitive approach, based on problem solving, which reduces the importance of the material used but emphasises instead the need for developing learning strategies.

A needs analysis is often the recommended way of developing new courses and therefore choosing teaching material. This approach could be defended - although only to some extent - if one had the luxury of small coherent groups of learners sharing the same aim; we were faced instead with a system of French for almost all. Our students now come from twenty different engineering courses, from naval architecture and environmental engineers to those studying mechanical engineering or electronics. Just as the choice of material does not arise from a specific type of course, so the students' needs have to be assessed on a much broader basis. Their motivation is varied and ranges from the panic of facing a semester in a French Ecole d'Ingénieurs, with very little preparation time, to the possibility of going to France in three years time. For some, the study of a language is compulsory; for others, it is an elective. All of them have extremely heavy time-tables and very little time to devote to the study of French outside their three weekly hours. Finally, to cater for the various entrance qualifications, we offer five different levels, from beginners to advanced.

Basic characteristics of any relevant material.

There is no readily available material for such courses, and as we started from scratch with the intention of creating a specific course for engineers - not a course with specific objectives - the search for suitable material could not be dissociated from the task of establishing good teaching practice based on solid theoretical grounds. The material is not the most important aspect of the teaching-learning relation but it is, to a great extent, the most tangible aspect of any course. It links the learner, his needs and expectations, the tutor and his methodology, and the target language and the skills to be developed.

We found it impossible to dissociate the choice of material from the development of an overall teaching policy, and this paper will argue the case for the integration of the material within the whole teaching/learning process. Having established our constraints in terms of student numbers, staff availability and other unavoidable limitations, we tried to establish some general priorities which would give us guidelines as to the choice of relevant material.

Various experiments as far apart as China or Scotland have shown that the students' main priorities lie in the field of aural comprehension and oral expression followed by reading comprehension and, relatively far behind, written expression. The choice of material had to reflect these priorities. This point is illustrated, for instance, by a study carried out by Yang Ming (1990, 108) from the Institut des Langues Etrangères in Shanghai, an institution which prepares Chinese post-graduates to come and study in France, Yang Min states that

> Les besoins langagiers à l'oral sont globalement ressentis comme plus importants que ne le sont ceux à l'écrit.[1]

This points to a necessary characteristic of any chosen material; whether the input is oral, aural, audio-visual or written, it has to lend itself to a possible oral exploitation. This limits, for instance, the usefulness of recording physics or mathematics lectures in French as the language teacher is - in general - badly equipped to develop such sources orally in the language class. Yang Ming also stresses the importance of socio-cultural awareness and advocates the necessity of

constituer un micro-environnement francophone multimédiatique à l'intérieur des centres chinois permettant aux boursiers doctorants chinois d'apprendre à mieux gérer leur apprentissage et à connaître le milieu socio-culturel dans lequel ils sont appelés à s'insérer.[2]

Much research in sociolinguistics has highlighted the same point. The study of a language cannot be dissociated from its cultural aspects.Television news, items reflecting every day life in France, statistics on the French economy, the legal duration of holidays, the welfare state, to mention but a few, are all useful. It is important that the material chosen opens up on to the general environment of the target language, even when the group is homogeneous and will put the language to use under the same conditions.

When our students come back from a semester of studying in France, they always stress the importance of oral comprehension and expression, and they mention their attempts to develop efficient practical strategies in order to cope with the difficulty of not being native speakers. One of the most effective and necessary survival strategies was being able to ask questions before and after lectures and tutorials: finding out how much had been done before on a particular topic, asking for help, begging for previous hand-outs etc. Most of them were surprised by French approaches, details such as the number of decimals to be given in an answer, or by the particular form of short-hand developed in each Ecole d'Ingénieurs. They stress that knowing such details in advance is not essential; what is important is the awareness that there would be differences. Few had had great difficulties with written documents relevant to their own specialism. Relevant material is therefore not the type which would mirror what they already know but the type which would entice them to probe further and ask questions.

It is also important for the material to be different from the type of French most learners have already encountered at school or from what can be found in most language course-books. Some were actively discouraged from studying languages at school because they were "scientists"; some, with vivid memories of former failures, consider themselves as "not good" at languages. The material chosen has to present an image associated with their present interests and their status as students of engineering. Using audio-visual material on scientific discoveries, technical inventions, information on working conditions, current affairs etc., is a type of approach which helps to recreate a more positive image of the language and bridge the gap between their level of intelligence and their level of French.

Last but not least, given our many constraints in preparation time and staff availability, the material also has to be flexible, so that the same input can be used with various groups, although different levels of response are expected from the students. Any material input demanding total comprehension for it to make sense or which is too highly specific should not have high priority when selecting the content of the curriculum.

Emphasis on oral production, flexibility, socio-cultural and technical content, an image better suited to students' expectations, those characteristics are based on needs common both to our material constraints and to the type of students we are teaching.

Specific language or specific purposes?

Practical experiments carried out in various teaching centres are a useful pointer to what might constitute relevant material, but can linguistic theories help us to define what variety of language should be taught? This would facilitate the choice of the right type of material. How specific can a variety of language be? Is there or is there not a French for science and technology (FST) or an English for science and technology (EST)? On this question, experts in the field are divided. According to Halliday (1988, 1):

> Scientific English is a recognisable category and any speaker of English for whom it falls within the domain of experience knows it when he sees it or hears it.[3]

But according to Hutchinson and Waters (1980):

> The language used in technical education is not, except for a few examples of terminology, subject specific nor even specific to technical communication. Everyday language is used.[4]

A possible way of integrating authentic material into an engineers' course might well start by considering various theoretical approaches to the topic and see what can be kept, rejected, or adapted in the light of the general needs and constraints listed above.

A very short survey of French for specific purposes and English for specific objectives shows interesting developments that affect the kind of material used for such courses. First, on the heels of the *Français fondamental,* the *Français scientifique et technique* implied that there was such a reality as a specific type of French; lexical and structural analysis would define this particular type of language, and it would be easy to find or make up the relevant material corresponding to very precise criteria. This implied that scientific and technical French was a very well-defined entity not likely to undergo rapid change and that "scientific" and "technical" did not differ in range or nature. Scientific text analysis, as advocated by Barber (1962, 21-43)[5], focused on the occurrence or recurrence of certain verb forms, verb tenses etc. This type of analysis of authentic material was useful to decide which material is most representative of the learner's own specialism but it did not go very far to help solving the real problem of language acquisition. What then followed was called either the *"français fonctionnel"* or, *"l'enseignement fonctionnel du français",* an ambiguity which raised the question of whether it was the language that had to be functional or its teaching. It led to useful developments in the field of communicative-functional-notional approaches, opened up new teaching methodologies and imposed the use of authentic material. Both French and English research on language for specific purposes developed the notion of needs, which L. Porcher neatly summarised as being *"à la fois indispensable et dangereuse"*[6] as needs are subjective and can be subdivided into too many sub-needs.

Allen and Widdowson (1974, 74) stress the different kinds of speech act determined by scientific texts: "define, classify, generalise, explain, make hypotheses, draw conclusions"[7] and gives us a more solid basis as to what type of material to select. The notion of speech acts allows us, for instance, to break language tasks into more defined and easily manageable units and to free ourselves from the straight jacket of technical material .

One of the latest publications on French as a Foreign Language is called *Publics Spécifiques et Communication Spécialisée,* a revealing title which puts the emphasis on the user of the language as well as on its use, and on the interaction between users of the language. The emphasis has gone from the specific language being the centre piece of the whole process, to the methodology of teaching, and now to the users of the language.

Putting the learner first.

Each of these complementary, or even contradictory, theories has a possible bearing on the selection of material, either by underlining the nature of the language, the role of teaching methodology or, in a more recent stage, the importance of the learner. In the first case, the emphasis was very much on the language itself. This type of approach has been proved to be far too restrictive but is still seen as being useful by some students, such as those who are going to study in a French Ecole d'Ingénieurs as part of the Erasmus exchange. Unaware of any linguistic theories, outmoded or not, such students feel reassured if they are given a list, for instance, of the verbs most commonly found in French examination papers, or listen to extracts of "real" lectures. This type of material can be best prepared with the help of a concordance programme, as shown by Stevens (1991).[8]

The importance of subjective needs cannot be dismissed, as self-confidence is important, but this approach, which looks as if it could be immediately useful, may in fact be closer to the placebo effect than to an effective teaching strategy. On the other hand, we cannot ignore the necessity of a certain amount of specialised vocabulary. Research done at the Université Libre de Bruxelles (1989) shows a correlation between lexical competence and examination success or failure in chemistry examinations. However, the researchers add - and it is comforting for us as our students are not expected to reach a native level of competence

Les performances des deux populations francophone et non-francophone s'avèrent néanmoins plus proches qu'on aurait pu imaginer.[9]

To respect the students' desire for technical French, while opening up other perspectives, we concluded that a half-way measure would be adequate, and we decided to use video clips of scientific popularisation such as specialised television programmes, extracts from the news and corresponding reading material. This provides a certain amount of technical vocabulary and relevant language structures, and allows both tutors and students to be involved in speech acts closer to real communicative situations, where both parties have something to offer. This would not always be the case if what was under discussion was a lecture on fluid mechanics, or a piece of French studied for the sake of learning some specific aspect of the language. This type of material also alleviates the boredom factor which may arise from having to study in French exactly what has already been covered in English, a pitfall underlined by Roe (1981)[10].

Language courses should preserve their uniqueness, which is to arm learners to cope with the unexpected rather than to provide them with translations of fossilised situations; after all, even a lecture on calculus may, one hopes, have an unusual format or unpredictable moments, as Tarentino (1991) points out "Students...expect to come out of the foreign language course combat ready."[11].

Using audio-visual material

In dealing with this kind of semi-technical material, the tutor is far from holding all the cards as the visual stimulus of videos incites the learners to draw from their own knowledge of the subject or to risk some explanation. This can place the tutor in a position where he has to learn something from his students and real communication can be established. A particular instance of this interaction was the occasion I thought we were shown tubes being welded, *"souder"*. In fact they were being bent into shape with a blow torch, *"couder"*. In the ensuing discussion, the students explained why, in that particular instance, "coudage" rather than "soudure" was necessary; the discussion - not unusual with this type of material - led to a wealth of language activities going well beyond the limitations of technical vocabulary and into the realm of personal interaction involving, for instance, the delicate task of telling me, as politely as possible, that my suggestion about welding was stupid! The students were ready to put me right on the technical side while accepting my guidance on the ways to express their disagreement and to describe what was taking place.

Before watching a video clip, students can prepare themselves by making hypotheses about what they are going to see; watching the clip without the sound will provoke a demand for the missing "tools". Such an approach has its drawbacks, as the tutor has to come well prepared but not set in his ways! Video clips provide a good basis for note taking, and a final showing of the clip, again without the sound, can be used to develop students' presentational skills. In this way, progress accomplished since the various hypotheses of the first viewing stage stands out clearly and contributes to a welcome sense of immediate achievement.

Scientific popularisation in an audio visual or written form has proved to be a very workable half-way measure between technical and general French. Technical vocabulary can be built on, typical verb forms can be practised, word formation analysed or whatever else has to be covered on the grammar front. Such material leads to communicative activities, but it can also be the basis for autonomous work on global or detailed comprehension if accompanied by worksheets. These worksheets must offer a variety of tasks of the true/false type, sequence order, multiple choice, or easy cloze exercises for intermediate levels progressing to note taking and transcription work for the more advanced students.

Audio-visual material does not need to be understood to the very last word to be worthwhile or effective. Determining various levels of response to an audio-visual stimulus is important. It is necessary to establish various steps:
- categorisation of the topic
- comprehension in general terms
- selection of certain information
- analysis of what is seen as difficult and why : too fast? Unknown vocabulary? No previous knowledge of the topic?
Whatever the material used, being able to recognise one's difficulties in dealing with it should be a positive part of the whole learning strategy.

Those who ask questions should be made to feel that they are succeeding as well as, if differently from, those who are able to provide the answers.

Towards greater autonomy in learning

Video extracts, coupled with reading passages on relevant topics, provide a good basis for autonomous learning provided they are supported by suitably graded worksheets, including step by step guidance, a vocabulary list and the correct answers. The following table is merely an indication of possible exercises and their degree of difficulty.

level	objective	nature of worksheet
1	General comprehension	Simple true /false statements Spotting words
2	More detailed comprehension	Multiple choice questions Cloze exercise Open-ended questions
3	In-depth comprehension	Completion of sentences Complex true/false statements Note-taking Transcription

Using a system of a cluster of video clips, for instance three sequences on a given topic, allows the learners to adopt one of several approaches, depending on their own way of learning; a longitudinal approach: working on all video clips at level one; then, having developed more confidence, they can proceed to the second level, and finally repeat the same process with the third. They can choose a vertical method, studying a video clip at level 1, then 2 and 3, then proceed in the same way with the other clips, trying to cover the ground more rapidly. They can take risks - an attitude to be strongly encouraged in language learners - and follow a diagonal pattern, clip 1 at level 1, then clip 2 at level 2, and finally clip 3 at the highest level of difficulty. As there is always the possibility of going back to start again at an easier level, the whole exercise does not carry a pass or fail penalty. This system allows for a greater flexibility of approach, a flexibility all the more necessary as the language tutor's perception of difficulty in technical or semi-technical areas could well be different from the learner's.

The worksheets should form an integral part of the material; they can be seen as auto-evaluation tests, allowing the learners to check how well they have coped with the task up to a precise point, or, and this is much more important, as formative evaluation allowing them to ascertain that what they knew, deducted or guessed is in fact correct and can be considered as a reliable basis for further work: This implies that the score to aim for has to be much higher than a simple pass mark. Worksheets should be presented as steps for easier and secure access rather than obstacles to be overcome.

"Hands on" approach.

Authentic material may also be taken, literally, as small pieces of apparatus used as prompts for various speech acts. Having to change the fuse in a plug can lead to:
- making hypotheses about the cause of the malfunction.
- describing how to open the plug and put it back together (using direct or indirect speech)
- defining the type of fuse etc.
- giving instructions
- writing a short report on what was done using relevant time connectors and appropriate verb forms.

In the same way, designing a garlic press or a nutcracker or explaining how they work will expand the learners' communicative skills.

Lego bricks and a general instruction to build a three-wheeled vehicle, or any other creation a given group may decide to tackle, will take the learners through:
- negotiation procedures: what to build?
- needs analysis: what type of bricks are needed?
- definition of the remit
- language research: relevant grammatical structures and lexis
- quantifying and qualifying
- expressions of doubt, contradiction, etc.

Assessment through trials of the completed vehicles can be followed by discussions on how to rectify problems. An assessment by each group of the merits of the various vehicles rounds off an entertaining and productive task. This can be followed up by other tasks, oral or written, of a more general nature such as advertising the vehicle, selling it or reporting its theft, etc. There is nothing new about teaching a language by "doing things" at school; it is probably less usual at university level. What is important is the fact that students should be made aware of the type of language knowledge they need to acquire or develop in order to perform this kind of task. There are marked advantages in using "mock" production processes in the language class rather than trying to develop the language within their technical course of studies, for instance, in a laboratory situation.

The ludic aspect of the mock task creates a distance between the learner and his task, and this breathing space removes the threat of failure (not building the best vehicle). By removing the necessity of completing the practical task successfully, the learner can concentrate on the language in a more relaxed frame of mind. It would not be the case in a technical laboratory where the primary task in hand - building something - would have to be completed satisfactorily irrespective of the accuracy of the language used.

Reading tasks from authentic material.

Reading tasks can be drawn from a variety of authentic sources, ranging from children and teenagers' magazines, articles from newspapers or extracts from technical magazines [12]. Engineering students tend to regard written passages in a far healthier way than students specialising in languages. They are less likely to regard those passages as a potential threat to their intelligence, or enemies which will defeat them if they fail to understand every single word. As they are less awed by the written word than students specialising in languages, more accustomed to treating reading material as another form of tool to be used to an end rather than as an end in itself, it is often easier to trigger various forms of interaction between them and the passage to be read. It is important for learners to have precise reading objectives and to be aware that different types of texts can be read differently.

Type of text	objective	reading strategy
Advertising (electric drill)	Finding precise information (e.g. size)	Rapid scanning: looking for figures
Magazine article (nuclear energy)	Finding arguments for and against	Several readings: looking for certain types of connectors.
French text-book (mechanics)	Gaining new information	Rapid scanning or step by step approach

Instructions for use (computer game rules)	Performing a precise task	Step by step and/or analysis of any visual aid (picture)
Short extracts from scientific magazines	Classifying them under proper headings Research purposes	Looking for "tell-tale" words. Proceeding by elimination
Cartoons	For pleasure	Getting maximum help from illustration

A grid can be worked out with the students themselves and every reading task and objective can be entered in a log kept by the students.

Reading strategies should be discussed before students start reading the passage as good preparation is essential. From recognising the topic to being able to classify, summarise, compare and generalise, the list of possible objectives is varied. Such a grid does not pretend to give any definitive guidelines but simply an indication of the type of preparation work which can be done with the learners. Cicurel (1991)[13] develops various interesting approaches.

The primary purpose of a grid is to give the learner practical guidance, but ultimately it is to help the learner to develop his own techniques when faced with any language task. Whatever the reading passage and its specific aim, students should always be encouraged to highlight important sentences, to circle meaningful connectors and to use mathematical devices, signs and symbols in the margin.

Problem solving: a common basis between languages and technology.

Learning a foreign language is, to a great extent, being able to solve numerous problems of comprehension or expression. Engineers are particularly well suited to learning languages in that spirit. Exploiting the type of problem-solving procedures they have already developed in other fields has many advantages, in particular the familiarity with known procedures which should take away the fear of the unknown.

But should we follow the assumption that there are universal concepts and methods as suggested by Widdowson? (1979, 24)

> The way English is used in science... may be more satisfactorily described ... as realisations of universal sets of concepts and methods or procedures which define disciplines or areas of enquiry independently of any particular language.[14]

Whether there are universal concepts or not, as argued by Swales (1985)[15], procedures and methods, if not concepts, do vary. Those variations might be irrelevant to theoreticians, what Bloomfield[16] refers to as the mere "dross of communication"; but, to students, they can be rather baffling. To give but one small example, the way the French do their long division, intrigues, puzzles and annoys British students, the only common factor between the two approaches being the result.

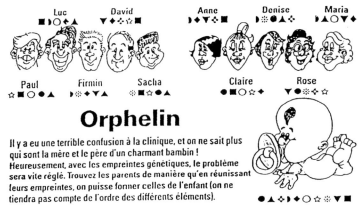

Orphelin

Il y a eu une terrible confusion à la clinique, et on ne sait plus qui sont la mère et le père d'un charmant bambin ! Heureusement, avec les empreintes génétiques, le problème sera vite réglé. Trouvez les parents de manière qu'en réunissant leurs empreintes, on puisse former celles de l'enfant (on ne tiendra pas compte de l'ordre des différents éléments).

Taking as a starting point that concepts and procedures are universal could lead to imposing a foreign frame of thought on the target language. The learner would then have to cope with two unknowns: the procedures and the language. Moreover, teaching a language should not aim at colonising the mind of the learner. To respect that potential difference, students should be able to set up their own procedures, defining them can be used as part of the language task. Let us consider the above puzzle (*Science et Vie Junior N° 37*), and how to solve it in a language class in the light of some extracts from the guidelines on writing a report given in one of our engineering departments. Most of the recommended steps could be adapted to a language task.

Engineering guidelines	language development
Introduction: lays out the general subject area of the experiment, the reasons for the experiment and the actual object of the experiment....	Define what has to be done. Analyse the problem. (several registers of language are possible from the familiar to the technical).
Apparatus: ....become familiar with names of manufacturers, finding and quoting serial numbers.....	Ability to name all the elements. Need to establish a consensus to describe the genetic prints
Procedure: Tell the readers exactly what you did. Use third person passive past tense (e.g. the engine was warmed through)	Describe what you did to solve the problem. tools: lexis acquisition : grammar structures
Results: Keep tidy and clear, do not drag them out for page after page	Develop the idea of language presentation, of style.
Discussion: This is the most important part of the report. It should contain a comprehensive critical survey of the experiment as a whole. You must ensure a continuous logical train of thought.	Discussion is the most important part. etc.... Expressing criticism Expressing links between cause and consequence etc.

Conclusion: should be straightforward, possibly with a statement of further work necessary.	Further discussion on the topic under discussion. and possible enlargement to other fields.

Students could be asked to produce a flowchart of the procedure they followed to complete the task and be expected to explain each step. Whether they have managed to discover or not that Luc and Rose are the happy parents, the real language work will revolve around the discussion of the methods (comparison, elimination) used to solve this particular problem.

The last task for the teacher could be to present the problem using the lexis and structures characteristic of a typical French problem

> "Etant donné un enfant dont les empreintes génétiques sont les suivantes.....connaissant également ... etc."

The task of the learners is not merely to solve the problem - in fact the pressure of having to come up with a perfect answer should not be emphasised to the detriment of the overall procedure - but to be able to define what they need to know and do in order to get to the result. This is already done in mathematics, for instance, where students are awarded points for the procedures as well as for the result. There is no reason why teaching a language should not follow this approach.

Experience has shown us that a multi-media approach gives the best result: videos, reading passages, oral and written tasks centred around the same topic seem to break barriers and improve the learner's knowledge of the language. To state that it is by accumulation seems too optimistic as everything is not retained; it might be better to say that learners seem to improve by slow sedimentation.

Whatever type of authentic material the teaching is based on, the emphasis should be shifted from the "what to teach?", "what with?" And even "why teach it?" approach to " who is learning and how?". Such a learner-centred approach poses the problem of integrating the role of the tutor differently into the whole process. A language should not be taught as if knowledge could be transferred wholesale from the teacher to the learner, the only problem being to limit the spillage during the transfer. Language cannot be reduced to more or less mechanical responses or to lists of specific vocabulary. The role of the tutor should be to determine a valid framework that will maximise the students' active input, to prepare the material, to set clear objectives and to develop formative evaluation exercises. It means more work in the background and a less visible presence. The consequence of using authentic material for specific purposes is that the tutor has less control over the linguistic form of the material and over the type of information it conveys. Being rather alien to most language tutors, authentic technical or semi-technical material forces the tutor to concentrate on the learner and his learning difficulties rather than on the difficulty of the material. A more unusual but healthier position.

References

Allen, J.P., Widdowson, H.G (1974) Teaching the Communicative Use of English, pp. 56-77, *English for Specific Purposes*, Longman.

Beacco, J.C, Darot, M. (1977) *Analyse de Discours et Lecture de Textes de Spécialité*, BELC.

Beacco, J.C. Lehmann, D. (eds.) (1990) *Publics Spécifiques et Communication Spécialisée* , Hachette.

Brumfit, C.J. (1981) Notional Syllabuses Revisited: A response *Applied Linguistics*, Vol II, N°1, pp.90-93.

Jacobi, D. (1987) *Textes et Images de la Vulgarisation Scientifique,* Peter Lang.

Holec, H. (1987) The Learner as Manager: Managing Learning or Managing to Learn in *Learner Strategies in Language Learning,* Prentice-Hall International.

Lehmann, D. (1980) Français Fonctionnel, Enseignement Fonctionnel du Français in *Ligne de Force du Renouveau Actuel en Didactique des Langues Etrangères,* pp.115-143, Clé International.

Lehmann, D. et al. (1981) *Lecture Fonctionnelle des Textes de Spécialité,* Didier.

Huddleston, R.D., Hudson, R.A.,Winter, R.A. & Henrici, E.O. (1968) *Sentences and Clause in Scientific English.* University College.

Hutchinson,T., Waters, A. (1987) *English for Specific Purposes.*, C.U.P.

Martin, A., Vigner, G. (1976) *Le Français Technique,* Hachette.

Martinez, C., Roux, P.Y. (1979) "Enseignement du Français à Usage Mathématique à des Non-Francophones", *Le Français dans le Monde* N°147, Hachette.

Munby, J. (1978) *Communicative Syllabus Design,* C.U.P.

Richterich, R. (1985) *Besoins Langagiers et Objectifs d'Apprentissage,* Hachette.

Trimble, L. (1985): *English for Science and Technology: a Discourse Approach,* C.U.P.

Vigner, G. (1979) *Lire: du Texte au Sens,* Clé International.

Vigner, G. (1981) *Didactique Fonctionnelle du Français,* Hachette.

Widdowson, H.G. (1983) *Learning Purpose and Language Use,* Oxford University Press.

Notes

1. Ming Yang (1990) La Préformation Linguistique des Boursiers Scientifiques Chinois in *Publics Spécifiques et Communication Spécialisée,* Hachette, p.108.

2. Ibid., p.109.

3. Halliday, M.A.K. (1988), On the Language of Physical Science, in *Registers of Written English: Situational Factors and Linguistic Features*, p.1.

4. Hutchinson,T. & Waters, A. (1980) "ESP at the Crossroads", *English for Specific Purposes Newsletter*, 36, pp.1-3.

5. Barber, C.L. (1962) "Some Measurable Characteristics of Modern Scientific Prose", in Almquist and Wilsell (eds.), *Contributions to English Syntax and Philology*, pp.21-43.

6. Quoted in Lehmann, D.(1990) "Avons-Nous Toujours Besoin de Besoins Langagiers?", *Publics Spécifiques et Communication Spécialisée*, pp.81-7.

7. Allen, J.P. & Widdowson, H.G. (1979) *Explorations in Applied Linguistics*, Oxford University Press, p.74.

8. Stevens, V. (1991) "Classroom Concordancing: Vocabulary Materials Derived from Relevant, Authentic Text", *English for Specific Purposes*, Vol 10 (1), pp.35-46.

9. Dalcq, A.E., Van Raemdonck, D., Wilmet, B. (1989) *Le Français et les Sciences*, Duculot, p.10.

10. Roe, J.P. (1981) "English for Academic Purposes ou l'Anglais Enseigné dans les Etudes Supérieures: un Guide pour le Débutant", *Etudes de Linguistique Appliquée*, 43, pp.124-135.

11. Tarantino, M. (1991) "English for Science and Technology: a Quest for Legitimacy", *English for Specific Purposes*, Vol 10, p.10.

12. Among the possible sources, in order of difficulty: *Okapi*, *Phosphore*, the scientific page of the *Figaro*, *Sciences et Vie Junior*, *Science et Vie*, *Science et Vie Economie*, etc.

13. Cicurel, F. (1991) *Lectures Interactives en Langue Etrangère*, Hachette.

14. Widdowson, H.G.(1979) *Explorations in Applied Linguistics*, Oxford University Press, p.24.

15. Swales, J. (1985) *Episodes in ESP*, Pergamon Press.

16. Bloomfield, L. (1939), "Linguistic Aspects of Science", *International Encyclopedia of Unified Science*, Chicago Press, I (4), pp.1-59.

Integrating Content and Context: Cultural Competence, Authentic Materials and Audience Design

Nigel Armstrong and Geoffrey Hare, University of Newcastle upon Tyne

Introduction

One of the topics that has concerned language teachers adopting communicative approaches in recent years is the relation of language and content within degree level language teaching syllabuses. As teachers and syllabus designers they have struggled to decide the extent to which language learning and the study of content areas featuring on their languages degree course can or should be integrated. Some, having decided in principle that language and content *should* be integrated, have then been faced with the problem of *how* this can be effectively or satisfactorily achieved. The debate has involved the issues of authentic materials and cultural (or cross-cultural) competence. This paper proposes to review some of the issues partly in the light of experience provided by courses concerned with written texts taught in the University of Newcastle upon Tyne.

The fact that a traditional (and successful) lang./lit. department of French like our neighbour Durham, for example, should, in 1991, have decided to teach a substantial portion of their content work through the medium of French indicates that something has changed in Britain's university French Studies departments. The debate over teaching the content in the language is not new; it was a live one, at least in Leeds Polytechnic's Department of Law, Languages and Economics twenty years ago, when new CNAA language degree syllabuses were in the process of creation. It must have surfaced from time to time in other departments long before that, with comparisons being drawn with continental practice. In the early seventies ideas about teaching through the medium of the foreign language were very much in the air, even though not many of us would have been aware of the recent writings of Hymes and Halliday, or Candlin and Widdowson[1]. At least their names were never mentioned. This did not stop us having strong views on the issue. The argument was often looked at then, as it is sometimes expressed now, from the point of view of the effects on content study. One of the central objections to "doing the content in the language" was the perceived danger of diluting the intellectual level of the content study, whether literature, politics or society. The supporters of "doing it in the language" often argued that such a loss was more than compensated for by the improvement in the students' command of the practical language.

The argument which advocates the integration of language and content remains today essentially that which was outlined above, although its proponents now usually underpin it with more sophisticated reference to studies of second language acquisition. However, the basis of the argument still centres on the beneficial effects of the *bain linguistique*, although this phrase will nowadays be used less than "rich linguistic environment". The study of aspects of the syllabus such as literature or history or area studies through the medium of French is often justified by reference to the communicative value of practice in reading, writing, listening and speaking in the foreign language around a topic, the set of activities being susceptible to definition in notional-functional terms. These arguments have been transformed then into ones which may be summed up as the philosophy of teaching the language through communication.

This debate remains active, and it is not our concern here to attempt to resolve it. This article is not really concerned with "doing everything in French", but rather with classes devoted to language (rather than content) and how to make them more effective. However, it seems appropriate to state explicitly at this point that we have adopted as the framework for our discussion the second, integrative approach, in full knowledge of its status as a *parti pris*. We hope that the arguments developed in this article will justify this decision.

Language, Content, and Cultural Competence

Looked at from a point of view which puts the stress firmly on the language, another set of arguments has gained currency over the last few years. These arguments view study of the foreign culture and society as an integral and unavoidable part of foreign language acquisition, but the content study is seen as subsidiary to the primary aim of language acquisition. Rather than starting from the position that there is some pre-determined content study already on the syllabus, the need for content study and its nature and scope are derived from the fundamental objective of language learning, of developing to the utmost the language skills of the learner. The assumption is that language is not fully comprehensible if divorced from a knowledge of the cultural and social context in which the language is used. The earlier approach (teaching the content through the language to improve the language skills) is less specific about ultimate aims. It invites the question *"Ecrire et parler, oui, mais pour quoi faire?"* The second approach, on the other hand, is quite clear about its aims, which are instrumental and usually quite explicit: the approach is designed to produce graduates who are conversant with the workings of the foreign society, while being able to operate effectively in the foreign language in communication with their French counterparts[2]. An extension of this aim is sometimes expressed as the ability to mediate between two linguistic communities. Whereas the previous approach could be termed as language through communication, this one is more ambitious: it attempts to teach communication through language.

The terms cultural competence and, sometimes, cross-cultural competence have been used to refer to one of the major desirable learning outcomes of this approach. The justification for the approach is derived from a particular view of the nature of language. The argument runs that using language in real situations involves an awareness of the socio-cultural dimension of the interaction. Since linguistic variation occurs according to social context and relationship with the interlocutor, language has to be used not only correctly (from the point of view of grammar or pronunciation), but also appropriately. By appropriately we mean with due regard, for example, to the level of formality/informality of the relationship between the speakers, since language is one of the key ways in which one expresses aspects of politeness, deference, relevance, emotions and so on. This sociolinguistic competence (as Canale and Swain[3] dubbed it, as distinct from the other three communicative skills of grammatical competence, discourse competence, and strategic competence) can only be learnt at the same time as learning the conventions of appropriate behaviour, i.e. cultural practices, which, since they are socially constructed, vary from culture to culture, and cannot be taken for granted even between West European cultures. For example, it has been argued that there are important differences between the French and (British) English strategies for disagreeing: whereas educated English native speakers tend to mitigate disagreements ("*Yes, that seems like a good idea, but on the other hand ...*"), equivalent French native speakers are more likely to by-pass the mitigating statement ("*Non, je ne suis pas d'accord*")[4]. The English learner of French has therefore not only to learn a number of linguistic realisations for expressing disagreement, but also has to learn to be more direct and forceful, if s/he wants to avoid being seen as evasive or not saying what s/he thinks. The opposite tendency might be the case when it comes to the formal written *lettre administrative*, where the English learner of French has to learn to become what from the English perspective seems over-polite, "flowery" or pompous, if s/he wishes to avoid being read as curt or disrespectful.

Taking on board this cross-cultural dimension has implications for foreign language learning syllabuses. When Lodge affirmed in 1985[5] that progress in Honours degree language syllabuses would involve an expansion of the range of varieties of French that a student can cope with (actively and receptively), he was also implying an extension of the social and cultural knowledge of the student. Increased familiarity with a greater number of the micro-cultures that go to make up a national culture might include for example the culture of business relations and a language variety associated with it, the business letter. Other examples could include the micro-culture of the academic world and the academic article, or media culture such as reading the local press with its mix of contents from *petites annonces* to *faits divers*. To take spoken language examples, it might be appropriate to choose from the business world the formal presentation (or *exposé*) to one's hierarchical superiors, or perhaps dinner-table conversation from the micro-culture of middle class socialising. What is probably only rarely included, to take an extreme example, is the chat-up line from the youth culture of sexual relationships. The written variety corresponding to the latter, since the love-letter has practically ceased to exist, might nowadays be definable by a study of Minitel *messageries*.

The range of language varieties is not infinite, but it is quite wide. Even in their own culture, however, from this wide range, individuals have only a number of varieties at their disposal, depending on their profession, the range of their social networks and their cultural background. The syllabus designer has to make choices about the range of social and cultural knowledge (and so of language varieties) students need to be proficient in. These choices can be made both in terms of the dominant micro-cultures in the linguistic community being studied, and/or according to any purposes or needs specific to the learner. In many courses where this approach has been pursued, the choice seems to have been influenced by the knowledge that students are being sent out into the world to work in graduate-type professional occupations in business or administration, and therefore would need to know a lot about the culture of management and business, international trade, public policy and administration, and government. Hence the choice of content courses on the macro- and micro-economy, society and politics of the linguistic community concerned. With more and more self-access courses and autonomous learning being talked about, there may be more scope for learners being given more freedom in defining the range of language variety and range of socio-cultural knowledge making up their course. After all, the communicative approach has always had a more learner-centred design than earlier approaches.

Authenticity

If one accepts the need to become familiar with the micro-culture corresponding to the language variety the learner is seeking to become proficient in, then it would follow that one needs to study authentic examples of utterances or texts produced in the relevant context. It is no accident that for practitioners of the communicative approach one of the buzz words has been "authentic", as in "authentic materials", which have become an integral part of teaching methods and activities and learning strategies. For instance, Brumfit's review of nine characteristics of the communicative approach includes "a concern for authentic materials", as part of the wider concern for realistic contexts for the presentation of language items[6]. His working definition of authentic materials seems a good one: "materials not intended for language teaching purposes at all" (one might add: "originally"). Another similar acceptance of the term when applied to written language is "non-edited texts", as opposed to texts specially written or simplified for language learning purposes, such as simple readers or "*textes en français facile*". Simplified materials do, of course, often find a place in the language learning classroom, especially in the early stages of learning, as a preparation for the learner's eventual control of authentic texts.

Plainly, however, the category "authentic text" is not a monolithic one, and language learners need to devise different strategies in order to respond to different types of text. Cicurel[7] proposes a classification of authentic written texts into five broad groups:

- media texts
- texts in the everyday environment
- letters
- professional (i.e. work-related) texts
- literary texts

Let us look in turn at each of Cicurel's categories. In responding to texts from newspapers and magazines, learners need to know how they derive some of their form and meaning from their physical context within the issue (prominence, location under a particular rubric etc.), but they also often fit into a time continuum and are part of on-going press (and TV/radio) coverage of a story which readers are assumed to be familiar with. An isolated text extracted from such a context poses difficulties for the language learner. On the other hand, knowledge of the layout of native-language newspapers is useful in allowing students to understand certain types of texts: *petites annonces* or an agony column, for example.

By texts from our everyday environment Cicurel means written signs in the street, menus in restaurants, posters on walls, packaging on goods, inscriptions on gravestones and so on. Such writings are extremely varied, both in their *supports* and in the degree of attention the reader pays them in the normal course of events.

Letters, both formal and informal, are defined as parts of a dialogue, with reference to a before (*suite à notre conversation, j'ai bien reçu votre lettre*), and an after (*dans l'attente de recevoir, par retour de courrier*), and often with a single predominant communicative function (e.g. *s'excuser, inviter, réclamer, demander une information*).

The common denominator of writings dealt with at work (reports, articles, memos, books), is the relationship of the reader to the texts. They have a specialised lexis and reference to other texts and other knowledge. For the learner, in reading this category of text, referential problems are often greater than purely linguistic ones. The student's real world knowledge of the particular work context may well need strengthening therefore. Their other important feature, however, is that the text type and its organisational rules also help "top down" understanding. The text may be composed according to a recognisable format.

Finally, literary texts are of course also authentic, although historically, in higher education in Britain, "authentic texts" (often limited to newspaper or magazine articles) began to be used in foreign language classrooms as a replacement for exclusive reliance on literary extracts. The length of literary texts may pose a problem to learners, as may their reference to a culture the student may be unfamiliar with.

Cicurel's reminder of the variety of authentic written texts is a useful antidote to the historic concentration by language teachers on the newspaper extract as the archetypal authentic text. Within the context of our discussion of what is meant by "authenticity", it is interesting to see that her classification derives from her analysis of the different ways in which the reader approaches and responds to the text. Indeed, what could be regarded as more important than the "authenticity" of any *materials* is the "authenticity" of the reader's *response* to them, or of the *activity* (in communicative terms) performed upon them. Widdowson[8] in particular has questioned the notion of authenticity within the communicative approach. He sees authenticity as not residing in instances of language, but as a quality which is bestowed on them or created by the response of the receiver. As Alan Davies[9] has said: "It is not that a text is understood because it is authentic, but that it is authentic because it is understood." It is the learner who authenticates text. The ambiguity of the term authenticity comes from confusion between its use (a) to mean actually attested language produced by native speakers for a normal communicative purpose, and (b) "to refer to the communicative activity of the language user, to the engagement of interpretative procedures for making sense, even if these procedures are operating on and within textual data which are not authentic in the first sense"[10]. To avoid this ambiguity, Widdowson suggested we retain the term "authentic" to mean the activity (i.e. process) and use the term "genuine" to refer to attested instances of language (i.e. product). In teaching language for communication then, authentic communicative activities seem more important than the exclusive use of authentic or genuine texts.

The above distinction is relevant to an example taken from course materials and activities used in the University of Newcastle: Hare's collection of recordings of political scientists and politicians, *Parlons Sciences Po*[11]. The recordings do not fit the common definition of authentic materials, since the interviews were made for pedagogic purposes. They had no other original *raison d'être*, and the speakers knew at the time of the interviews that they were being recorded to be heard and studied by foreign learners of French. However, it may be argued that they are authenticated by the learner who uses them (as intended) as an introduction to the study of French politics. They fill an information gap which allows the student to speak or write about the topic having listened to them for the information and ideas they contain. The fact that the speakers are experts in their field makes the student all the more likely to view them as a real source of information. Concentration on the topic rather than the form gives communicative authenticity to the activity. This too has been a common theme among proponents of the communicative approach. "The teacher's focus ought to be on the content of the communication, as this will foster the acquisition of form" (Murray[12]). This echoes Krashen's ideas on comprehensible input: "focus on the message, not the form"[13]. The interviews are of course examples of "genuine" unscripted French, corresponding to the genre which in British French Departments is referred to as "*exposé*", and as such will serve as models for that speech act, when, in a further authentic activity a student is asked to report on his/her investigations into a related political topic.

However, the distinction between message and form, except perhaps at an elementary stage of language learning, appears artificial or at best rather fuzzy from the point of view of the communicative approach, whose essential aim may be argued to be the teaching of *contextualised* language. As stated above, this approach requires the teaching of sociolinguistic skills along with the purely linguistic, such as syntax and lexis. Indeed, it is arguable that at any stage of language learning beyond the elementary, one cannot reasonably ignore the social dimension when teaching linguistic skills without producing odd results (an example is provided below), since the extra-linguistic factors which shape a text influence every linguistic level - phonology, lexis, syntax, and the larger discourse units.

Context and Audience

If one accepts the need always to sensitise students to the social context surrounding a text or utterance, this process can be examined along the customary reception/production axis. Plainly, students need to know the provenance of an authentic text if they are to respond to it fully; further, as will be argued below, close linguistic scrutiny of a text in relation to its provenance will help production. But it is on the level of production that students most manifestly need to be made aware of the destination or "audience" of a text, for it is the audience that principally influences the way in which a writer produces or "designs" a text.

This notion of "audience design" was first formulated by Bell[14], in a paper which sought to demonstrate that it is principally the audience, in the sense of the addressee(s), that influences stylistic variation. Using the insights of the accommodation theory of social psychology, Bell marshalled a range of findings from sociolinguistic studies to support his arguments, which in essence are twofold: firstly, that the audience is the overriding factor influencing the choice of style (of speech, with which Bell was concerned; but of course the same arguments apply to written texts), and that all other factors, such as topic or the degree of attention paid to speech (monitoring), are subsidiary; and secondly, that stylistic variation "derives from and mirrors social variation"[15], such that the most formal styles will be drawn from the most prestigious social varieties; conversely, informal styles will derive from less prestigious varieties.

Clearly, the implications of audience design for the production of texts by students are, first, that students need to be aware of the audience or context to which they are addressing their text, and, second, that students must have access to the style of language appropriate to the target text.

To take the second point first, the relation between comprehension and production is important here, as suggested above. In a general sense, students need to be sensitised to the notions of social and stylistic variation, and to the fact that every text has a specific provenance. These seemingly unsurprising facts need to become clearly articulated in the student's mind. The fact that they often remain vague and inchoate goes far towards explaining the stylistic errors that students produce. Further, and more particularly, a close analysis of those linguistic features in a text which are governed by the sociolinguistic constraints upon it will manifestly be needed before analogous production can be expected of students.

The second need (chronologically) will be the definition of an authentic, or at least plausible, audience for whom the text is to be produced. Defining the audience in this way removes many of the difficulties which the convoluted teacher/student relationship tends to bring about when a student is required to produce a text. This sort of difficulty may be illustrated by the example of a piece of work produced in a first-year Honours *résumé* course taught at Newcastle, where students were required to write French-French summaries of newspaper articles. The lack of a specified audience produced one notably grotesque result on the level of anaphora, explicable by the fact that the student knew she was writing for a teacher who was familiar with the original text; whence the production of a secondary text which had little coherence independently of the original. The source text was prominently entitled "Implacable Chanel", and started thus:

> "Elle ne pouvait mourir qu'un dimanche. En semaine, on travaille. Et seule, dans sa chambre de l'hôtel Ritz ..."[16]

The student's version was entitled: "Summary for Mr Armstrong", and started: "Elle est morte un dimanche." Who had died was not mentioned. Teachers may of course wish to ignore this type of relatively subtle inadequacy when it emerges early on in a language course, where students are still struggling with the smaller linguistic units, but it seems legitimate to require of more advanced students the ability to produce an appropriate text, entirely or at least adequately adapted to its intended audience. The shortcoming on the teacher's part in this example was plainly his failure to require the students to write for an imagined audience who should be assumed to be ignorant of the source text, and this requirement seems axiomatic for all types of summary-writing. One might thus hypothesise a "null" or "default" audience[17] whose principal characteristic is ignorance of the original text. It is of course possible to specify more closely the intended audience for a text, arguably with more successful results, as the following example is intended to demonstrate.

Students following the second-year written language Honours course at Newcastle entitled *Traduction et stylistique* might typically be asked to summarise a *fait divers* from a *journal régional* or *local* for insertion in a similar newspaper in a neighbouring locality. The author and audience are specific: respectively journalist and sub-editor. This exercise requires the acquisition and production of the vocabulary surrounding the *fait divers*, as well as of certain syntactic and morphological features typical of this type of news text: for example, the contrasting use of the *passé simple* and *passé composé*, the use of the historic present, the use of a direct interrogative where the English reader would expect an indirect.

At another level, where the linguistic shades into the socio-cultural, the exercise introduces students to some of the discoursal features that characterise news texts[18]. For instance, the following exercise obliges students to balance in a news text the competing aspects of *negativity* and *proximity*; on the one hand, the axiom "no news is good news", implying as is does that only bad news is real news, reflects the typical reader's (deplorable?) interest in reading principally about negative events; on the other hand, with the exception of events which are marked in some other way, e.g. for *novelty* (their unusual aspect) or *superlativeness* (the large scale of the event), the interest of a news story diminishes in proportion to the reader's distance from it. The tension between the former two principles provides a firm framework which guides the student's choice as to what should be foregrounded (the negativity), and what left out or backgrounded (the features of proximity) in summarising the following text.

The instructions to the students were as follows:

Texte d'un fait divers.
Vous travaillez pour *Le Républicain lorrain*. Vous avez remarqué le fait divers suivant sur un télex d'une agence de presse. Il a déjà été repris par le journal régional *L'Alsace*. Vous voulez le faire paraître dans votre journal, mais le secrétaire de la rédaction vous dit que vous n'avez pas assez d'espace pour le texte entier. Il faut le réécrire en 100 mots, y compris le(s) titre(s).

Rappelez-vous que le texte que vous avez sous les yeux a été rédigé pour des lecteurs d'un journal local ou régional, et que vous écrivez pour un autre journal régional, dont les lecteurs connaissent sans doute moins bien l'Alsace, et/ou s'y intéressent moins.

Utilisez le micro-ordinateur pour réduire ce texte à 100 mots. Imprimez-le quand vous aurez terminé.

The text was the following :

Tentative de cambriolage en présence des clients à Altkirch

Un café saccagé, deux consommateurs hospitalisés

Une violente bagarre s'est soldée samedi soir dans un café d'Altkirch par deux blessés graves qui ont dû être transportés à l'hôpital du Moenchsberg à Mulhouse par l'ambulance des sapeurs-pompiers. Une bagarre qui n'a cependant rien à voir avec les rixes habituelles qui se produisent dans certains débits de boissons.

Il était environ 19h. Des clients, des retraités, sont attablés au café à l'Etoile (Chez Rudy) à la sortie d'Altkirch (vers Carspach). Un groupe de personnes entre: deux hommes, trois ou quatre femmes, une fillette. Ils s'attablent et consomment.

Le patron du café étant sorti, l'un des personnages se rend purement et simplement derrière le comptoir. Apparemment pour se servir en cigarettes. Pour les retraités, occupés à jouer aux cartes, le manège est insolite: ces individus sont inconnus. Pas de doute, les cigarettes ne sont qu'un prétexte. Effectivement c'est au tiroir-caisse que le personnage s'en prend.

Les retraités alertent le patron. La réaction est immédiate: les personnages, qui les témoins identifient formellement comme des gitans, déclenchent une violente bagarre à laquelle les femmes participent avec autant de violence que les hommes. Tables, chaises, verres, tout vole. A coups de bouteilles cassées, à coup de pied, ils s'en prennent au patron et aux clients. Deux de ceux-ci sont sérieusement blessés. Le café est totalement saccagé.

Les individus profitent de la surprise et de la mêlée pour prendre la fuite.

L'enquête de la gendarmerie d'Altkirch est en cours.[19]

One criticism of the above type of integrative exercise would state that one can never really create an audience-designed task which induces students to engage successfully in this kind of written role-play and thus lose their consciousness of the teacher as the real audience for the text. However, we would argue that a tightly framed exercise such as the one specified above, defining as it does very explicitly not only the putative author and *destinataire* of the text, but also to some extent the structure required, is capable of overriding in a large measure the awareness on the part of the student of the teacher's preponderant role; for even if one accepts the proposition that the addressee is indeed the primary influencing factor in the drafting of a text, a rather major qualification must equally be stated, namely that certain types of text are closely associated with certain types of audience. A journalist writing a story for his or her sub-editor will be closely constrained in terms of such textual properties as topic, order and emphasis. These are powerful constraints, and one might argue that by closely specifying to students a cluster of textual and extra-textual conditions bearing on the drafting of a piece, a suspension of disbelief on their part in respect of the intended audience may be achieved.

However, this rather mentalistic question is clearly unresolvable, and the proof of the pudding is in the eating. A reliable measure of the effectiveness of applying the principle of audience design to (say) summary-writing must be sought by examining the students' production; if they avoid certain errors of coherence and emphasis in performing the type of exercise exemplified above (the sorts of errors which characteristically appear when students write for a "default" audience), we may conclude that the constraints which the teacher has imposed and which the students have been obliged to respect have so framed their writing as to bring about a satisfactory result (an eatable pudding).

As noted above, the distinction between these constraints, whether linguistic or extra-linguistic, is not a sharp one; nor can we be sure of the primacy of any one constraint in directing students' production in the desired direction. We can, however, report that students' success in performing this type of exercise is in general greater than that achieved in the typical undirected summary.

The following summary of the Altkirch article was drafted in the class hour by two students who are not outstandingly weak or strong in written French:

UN CAFE SACCAGE - DEUX CONSOMMATEURS HOSPITALISES

Samedi, à 19h, il y avait une bagarre dans un café à Mulhouse.

Les clients réguliers jouent aux cartes et un groupe de personnes inconnus, formellement identifiés comme des gitans, entrent. Ils s'assoient. L'un des gitans va au comptoir sur le prétexte de prendre des cigarettes, mais il prend le tiroir-caisse.

Les autres clients alertent le patron, qui n'est pas là. Le résultat: une violente bagarre, deux clients sérieusement blessés, et un café totalement saccagé.

Dans la confusion, les voleurs ont fui. L'enquête de la gendarmerie d'Altkirch est en cours.

(We have let stand the small-unit errors and infelicities of agreement, tense etc., as being irrelevant to the present discussion.) On the level of textual coherence and emphasis, these students seem to have understood the need to foreground on the one hand the original text's negativity values, and on the other to background or delete its proximity values. The resulting text, we would argue, represents a fair attempt at carrying out the task required; the article is comprehensible without reference to the original, and contains a good balance of the requisite news values designed to engage the interest of the target audience.

It will be objected that this assessment is subjective and impressionistic, and we cannot but acknowledge this; a systematic appraisal of the exercise, involving the use of a control group, remains to be carried out.

However, an indirect indication of the value of the audience-designed approach may be found in a contrast between the results of the exercise described above (i.e. the students' production) and a translation of the following text which was required of the same students:

Une explosion embrase un restaurant et un immeuble de trois étages

Un homme brûlé vif, trois blessés hier à Mulhouse

Un homme de 61 ans, M. Justin Meyer, brûlé vif, et trois personnes blessés, dont une grièvement, tel est le triste bilan du très violent incendi.e.

qui, à la suite d'une forte explosion de gaz, a entièrement ravagé un restaurant 'La Romantica' et l'immeuble de trois étages qui l'abritait, hier après-midi, rue Hugwald, à Mulhouse.

Un bilan auquel il importe de rajouter quatre sapeurs-pompiers intoxiqués (sans gravité finalement) par la fumée et la terrible chaleur qu'ils ont eue à affronter...[20]

Most students reproduced the rather prolix style of the French text in their English translation, for example by translating *tel est le triste bilan* more or less literally, and the result was an unconvincing piece of news text. This result might have been avoided by specifying a more or less plausible audience, for instance the readers of the local paper in Mulhouse's twin town, and imposing a word-limit, again in the interests of balancing negativity and proximity; the students would also need to be made aware of the fact that newspaper French seems in general to be more wordy than the English equivalent.

An exercise from the same course which contrasts with the orthodox *version* is an extended group translation project[21]. To judge from students' responses to questionnaires, their motivation as perceived by the teachers concerned, and more demonstrably from the quality of the work the students produced, this has been one of the most successful activities in the second year Honours language course over the last couple of years. Now, written translation is not the first activity one thinks of when considering matters of authenticity or indeed the communicative approach in general. However, it can be presented within a communicative framework. Students are asked to work on either a chapter of a non-fiction book about an aspect of contemporary France or an academic article on a topic they are studying as part of their content courses. They are asked to translate it into English as if for publication, bearing in mind the intended audience. Discussion of the characteristics and needs of an "authentic" audience is one of the keys to the exercise, since, as noted above, the cultural knowledge of the potential readers will need constantly to be taken into account by the translator, given that s/he is writing for that audience as a cross-cultural communicator. Certain French culture-bound items will have to be explained or paraphrased for the English reader. On the other hand, where the audience (e.g. for a scholarly article on linguistics) can be assumed to share an academic culture, the translator has to make a judgement about what is shared terminology and what needs a cross-cultural gloss. Another major requirement is of course the acquisition of the register of similar English text types.

A further, major advantage which accrues from the teaching of audience-designed writing stems, paradoxically, from the need to dispel the typical student's ignorance of the referential conditions or the practical realities surrounding the drafting of any more or less specialised piece of writing. Students of 18-20 years of age have comparatively little real-world knowledge, especially of the work-place. Reference was made above to the need to prepare students for the journalistic summary exercise by sensitising them to certain aspects of the newsroom, i.e. the hierarchy of journalists, and to certain news values which characterise the typical piece of "hard news". This type of preparation might be considered to operate on a rather trivial level of cognition, but we would assert that, on the contrary, any process of instruction which sensitises students to the way in which journalists (and other authors) mediate aspects of the world through language constitutes an important part of the process of a liberal education; to resume the example discussed above, that of the news values which characterise any piece of journalism, one can argue that an awareness of these should form part of any educated person's *bagage*, for they help the informed reader to analyse the distorting effect which any text operates upon the fragment of referential information (the piece of reality) with which it is concerned. This is not a trivial insight, and it can, and indeed must, be communicated to students through the teaching of audience-designed manipulation of a news text - at first sight a purely linguistic exercise.

Conclusions

We have attempted in this article to define, in the light of current theories of L2 acquisition and of stylistic variation, what seem to us to be the aims and advantages of communicative language teaching through the use of authentic materials, and to illustrate how their application in practice may resolve certain difficulties inherent in the production of non-contextualised linguistic output. Our judgements on the success of this latter enterprise are necessarily rather impressionistic, although, as noted above, some evidence exists, in the form of students' responses and enhanced production, to support theoretical assumptions (satisfying in themselves) on the preferability of attempting wherever possible to elicit contextualised linguistic production. A systematic appraisal of the effectiveness of or "value-added" by the audience-designed approach remains to be undertaken.

Does the above discussion allow us to add anything to the debate over the use of authentic texts in the communicative language class? First, authentic texts were defined as texts not originally intended for language teaching purposes at all. Second, they lost authenticity if they were edited or simplified, and therefore they should remain, at least for advanced students, in their original form with their original presentation (e.g. with original typeface, and any accompanying illustrations). The new audience's or learner's reception of them is an additional factor in conferring authenticity on texts. We would add that another condition is that a text's provenance needs to be made fully explicit. The original context of reception and production would seem to be an essential parameter in understanding what the text is saying and how it is saying it. Regarding the student's subsequent production, studying the sociolinguistic context of model texts in relation to their linguistic features is a necessary prerequisite to improving the appropriacy of the student's own French as communication; it also forms part of the high-order educative process, contributing as it does to a fuller understanding on the student's part of the way in which writers mediate the world through language.

Finally, this latter point is worth developing more fully. The undergraduate's understanding of the real world outside the classroom seems to be, at one and the same time, a key limitation on the authenticity and success of contextualised exercises and a justification for doing them, in so far as there are good general educational reasons for trying to remedy the student's lack of real-world knowledge. The context of the newsroom of a local newspaper, the example used above, does make certain unusual demands on students in terms of taking on a role which is foreign to their experience. The rules of the game can be fairly quickly spelled out, however. Other contexts and roles might be too distant from their experience, especially if, instead of a summary of a given text, a free composition is required: how would the average undergraduate cope with the task of writing a memorandum as a CGT délégué(e) syndical(e) to the PDG of a PMI in textiles asking for equal pay for women working on the shop floor and men working in the stores? (This is not so far-fetched as never to be likely to appear on an undergraduate syllabus.) The student would probably couch the argument in academic, moral, even philosophical terms of right and wrong. There are two difficulties (at least) in such an exercise, both involving leaps of the imagination on the part of the student: the difficulty of putting herself into the shoes of the shop-steward representing real workers; and the difficulty of second-guessing the response of an employer to certain arguments. If not based on some real experience of working life, the written product is unlikely to be successful. The designer of contextualised written exercises must always bear in mind therefore that the roles advanced students of language can be asked to play are very restricted, if one wishes to attain some authenticity of response. Most undergraduates will find it difficult to stray from their own persona, given their restricted experience of life. We have all seen the much more informed and realistic response of the odd 40 or 50 year old mature student in such written exercises. We cannot expect the same sophisticated world view from most 20 year olds, enabling them to take on a wide range of roles or to imagine the response of a range of destinataires. In this light, then, the roles of writer and addressee in such exercises need to be chosen (and described or defined) very carefully.

However, having issued this pedagogical health warning, we come back to the notion that contextualisation is not just an artificial exercise done for theoretical reasons, but is, in its modest way, part of a wider education, preparing young people for the real world, where language is not used just for academic purposes in a disinterested or objective ideational mode, but by interested parties for purposes of persuasion. In real life, where a letter has to be written on behalf of workers to an employer, the writer has to learn to angle arguments to the addressee's self-interest. From this extrinsic perspective then, one justification of contextualised role-play exercises is that they dispel students' naiveté about how, in the real world, people manipulate others by means of language.

Notes

1. See C. Brumfit (Spring 1991) "Teaching Communicative Competence", *Franco-British Studies*, 11, pp.1-9, for a brief history of ideas on communicative competence.

2. See D. Ager and L. Hantrais (1986) "Communicative ability in University French", in M. Bate and G. Hare (eds), *Communicative approaches in French in higher education*. Salford, AFLS.

3. M. Canale and M. Swain (1979) "Theoretical bases of communicative approaches to second-language teaching and testing", *Applied Linguistics*, 1, 1, pp.1-47.

4. J. Thornborrow (Spring 1991) "Language in use: teaching cross-cultural competence", *Franco-British Studies*, 11, pp.83-92.

5. A. Lodge (1984) "What are we doing in Modern Languages today?", *Bradford Occasional Papers*, No. 5, pp.3-25.

6. C. Brumfit, *op. cit.*, p.3.

7. F. Cicurel (1991) *Lectures interactives en langue étrangère*, pp.21-36, Paris, Hachette.

8. H. Widdowson (1983) *Learning purposes and language use*, Oxford, OUP, p.30.

9. A. Davies (1984) "Simple, simplified and simplification: what is authentic?", in J. C. Anderson and A. H. Urquhart (eds.), *Reading in a foreign language*, London, Longman, p.192.

10. Widdowson, *ibid.*

11. G. Hare (1982) *Parlons Sciences Po*, Paris, British Institute in Paris, and (1989) *Parlons Sciences Po '89. Introduction à l'étude de la vie politique française*, Paris, British Institute in Paris.

12. I. Murray (1983) "New approaches: old problems", *British Journal of Language Teaching*, 21 (3), pp.135-142.

13. S. Krashen (1982) "Principles and practice in second-language teaching", in *Pergamon Institute of English: Collection of Krashen's papers*. Quoted in Murray, *op. cit.*

14. A. Bell (1984) "Language style as audience design", *Language in Society*, 13, 2, pp.145-204.

15. Bell, *op. cit.*, p.153.

16. Françoise Giroud (1971) "Implacable Chanel", *L'Express*, 1019, (18 janvier 1971), reproduced in Ross Steele (ed.) (1977), *Françoise Giroud, Jean-Jacques Servan-Schreiber dans l'Express*, Didier, p.29.

17. We owe these terms to our colleague Hugh Dauncey. We should also like to thank Tony Lodge, also of Newcastle University, for his useful comments on the typescript.

18. Cf. A. Bell (1991) *The Language of News Media* (Oxford, Blackwell), pp.156-158, for a discussion of the extra-linguistic factors which shape news stories.

19. *L'Alsace lundi* (8 juillet 1985), 8.

20. *L'Alsace lundi*, *ibid.*

21. For a description of this course see G.E. Hare, "Transferable Personal Skills, Communicative language teaching and Graduate Employment prospects after 1992", in David Staquet and Klaus Zeyringer (eds.) (1992), *Les Langues: Pivot du nouvel espace économique européen (17e colloque annuel de l'Association Internationale Langues et Economie, Angers, IPLV, 10-11/10/1991)*, Nottingham, Praetorius Press, pp.185-99.

Integrating the Year Abroad

Gordon Inkster, Lancaster University

"A degree in Modern Languages is a sandwich course and the meat is the year abroad" (Evans, 1988, 42)

1. Changes

Twenty years ago Colin Evans' assertion was clearly untrue. The "statutory year abroad" was often an academically peripheral and stand-alone experience in every sense, sometimes a mere voluntary option. Students were despatched overseas, often unprepared and largely unsupervised. Many pursued courses for which they were ill-suited and which had at best a tangential bearing on their past or subsequent degree syllabus. Others were assistants, whose experiences, good or ill, proved sufficiently challenging to preclude much formal study beyond perhaps a first reading of the following year's set texts. In both cases it was hoped that a nine-month immersion in French life would prove sufficient gestation to bring forth a raucously healthy infant-Finalist.

The notion that linguistic performance would inevitably be transformed for the better by the vagaries of some such painless osmotic process has been largely eradicated. Nor do many now imagine that the inadequacies of our teaching and the cracks in our language curriculum can be remedied by the deluge of authenticity to which they would be exposed for a quarter of their course.

The student habit of referring to a "year out" continued to reinforce the impression that the period is at best an escape from their other studies, at worst a purgatory to be endured:

"I sentence you to one year abroad"...A "Year abroad" or "134 working days" - I couldn't decide which sounded the longer sentence. It wasn't so much that I hated my new life, it was just that I'd rather have been back at university ... (Anon, 1988)

Sometimes it worked, of course, and a pedagogy promoting an "Outward Bound" spirit of survival has undeniable merits. Such nakedly character-building practices are nonetheless inefficient and ipso facto ill-suited to both current priorities and the needs of the present generation of students. Numerous factors supervening in the past two decades have made it less probable that students will "tough out" the experience profitably and uncomplainingly. Prominent amongst these has been students' intensified concern to improve their own employability. It is this, together with an overall recognition of the inevitable Europeanization of job markets, that has impressed upon even the most "purist"of staff the need to maximize the effectiveness of the year abroad experience by enmeshing it more firmly into the remainder of the degree.

For students, the value of European experience and study has been foregrounded by the example of their immediate predecessors, frequently driven, as much by personal preference as by the vagaries of the market, to establish themselves overseas after graduation. The swing to combined schemes, especially those linking a language and a more directly vocational discipline, has also highlighted the need to practise the other discipline within its overseas context.

Most significantly, we no longer see competence and performance in language, and especially in the spoken language and its familiar registers, as at best a secondary component of language degree schemes. It is this above all that encourages us to see the year abroad no longer as peripheral, but rather the central component in the language degree scheme. Our task then becomes not one of adapting the year abroad to the remainder of the syllabus, but more fruitfully that of finding ways in which the syllabus can contribute to, and later build upon, different varieties of overseas experience.

2. Preparation

Preparation for overseas study has hitherto reflected the peripheral curricular status it seemed to enjoy. It has been largely a sudden-death affair, concentrating largely on bureaucratic procedures and sometimes elements of EFL. The former polytechnics were especially sensitive to the limitations of such an approach from an early date, and often provided booklets covering a range of problems and lacunae identified by former students. In the case of university exchanges these were supplemented by pages of documentation on the specific institution the student was to attend.

Byram's survey covered all categories of HEFC institution, albeit in seriously skewed proportions: universities (34%), Oxbridge colleges (37%), former polytechnics (18%) and HE colleges (11%). It found a majority (67%) of institutions offered preparatory courses for assistants, while only 33% provided anything similar for those in placements or enrolled in universities. Most courses were brief and took place shortly before departure. (Byram, 1988, 13). In such circumstances they may well be as much a source of apprehension as of reassurance, highlighting likely problems at the very moment when students feel most vulnerable.(See Rouxeville and Windsor, 1992))

If, however, the year abroad is indeed the kernel of the degree, we might rather consider how all of the courses followed in the year prior to departure might be geared to enriching it. Such a perspective, were it achievable, would have the immeasurable benefit of focussing student's minds on their course at a time when the excitement of entering university has evaporated and before the imminence of Finals concentrates the mind. This is a period of especial uncertainty for language students, often frustrated by their apparent lack of progress, unsure of what the next year holds and fearful of losing their friends.

Such students' preparatory requirements might be categorized as:

Discipline-based
Linguistic
Socio-cultural
Affective

It is immediately clear that the greater part of our effort during their year prior to departure overseas is dedicated to pursuing the first of these: those same literary, historical, marketing, accounting or other units that they might follow were they not going to France. Given indeed that the teaching of these frequently takes place in groups that include other categories of student this is more easily avoided when significant numbers of students are following an integrated syllabus. There are nonetheless steps that can be taken to focus such parts of *any* syllabus more directly on similar courses that may be followed in the French context. The case for individuation of learning and assessment by project work, for example, is very strong in this context, as are all measures favouring interaction and collaboration with French students pursuing those same disciplines on the learner's home campus.

This is especially important for those not studying traditional arts disciplines. Adding a language component to the accountancy or chemical engineering is not merely throwing in one further skill to be acquired. Students who have chosen combined degree schemes where language is a significant element inevitably come to recognize, that operating in a foreign context requires a "cultural competence" which must be reflected in all of their other studies[1].

There is a powerful case here for promoting the staff exchanges that can be partially supported by COMETT and ERASMUS funds. Students who are taught French law, accountancy, history or linguistics by native practitioners of these disciplines readily view them as purveyors of up-to-date information, an expectation no doubt sometimes ill-founded ... The undeniable value of such visitors is the example of relevant French professional attitudes and practices that they inevitably bring to their teaching, perhaps at times unwittingly. Where class sizes allow they can also contribute to special-purpose language teaching, a healthy reminder that not only language-teachers teach language.

Language units too can clearly generate increased motivation if their content is aimed more directly at the real-world activities that will have to be faced a year later. The notion that a few hours or weeks suffice for this is an echo from the past. All students gain from mastering the verbal and social niceties of letter-writing and preparing French CVs early in the year, especially those applying for placements. Coping with new registers of the spoken language, from adolescent slang to the political harangue needs lengthier and more concentrated practice than the summer term can provide.In this respect video-based courses like *Lyon à la une*, and more especially Renee Birks' *Une Vie d'étudiant* are vivid encounters with pertinent authenticity. The formal documents that will be encountered: *permis de séjour, immatriculation à la sécurité sociale, polices d'assurance, carte d'étudiant, relevé d'identité bancaire*, can also with imagination all be turned entertainingly into much more than lessons in bureaucratic jargon.

Greater command of the relevant language domains may be a necessary prelude to developing a greater understanding of French life-styles, but it is patently not a sufficient one. Accounts of negative student experiences in France often stress the boredom of domesticated small-town living and the brusque indifference of officialdom, the daily and weekly routines, strikes, overflowing lecture-theatres. For those who abandon their stay abroad early encounters with these are often what prove damning.

Minimising the shock of life without buses or discos or mixing with students who live with their parents is perhaps not best achieved within the formal curriculum at all. Merely describing the problems and suggesting solutions belatedly can prove both tedious and counter-productive. The same applies to well-intentioned efforts to outline the intricacies of winning reimbursement for prescriptions: often at best a wasted effort if it merely exacerbates rapidly surfacing apprehensiveness.

Promoting the attitudinal changes needed to cope with French life is far better approached by longer-term stratagems, and not necessarily within the curriculum. Anything that can be done to encourage social interchange with French students of similar age and circumstances is of far greater value than harangues by our middle-aged selves. Departmental heads may be reluctant to fund socialising with local *assistants*, yet this can have genuine academic rewards if friendships thus established contribute to an easier insertion into French routines.

By its mere topicality satellite television has much to offer in this context, but then so does radio, yet British students have proved curiously hostile to listening to *France-Inter* at home rather than Radio One. Written exchanges with French students of English via JANET and EARN or Internet Relay Chat, precisely because they are live and interactive, offer more exciting new prospects for exploring each other's life-styles and institutions, a practice many students pursue voluntarily via monolingual electronic bulletin boards. The uninhibited character of the correspondence that this new medium encourages is startling, but its contribution to collaborative learning undeniable. It already introduces our students to transatlantic lifestyles. With guidance it can be used to help them introduce themselves to French civilisation, and this will become easier with the forthcoming establishment of a French university network analogous to our own.

Teaching students and encouraging them to learn is usually easier than keeping them happy. Yet it is overwhelmingly the personal and affective domain that determines whether departing students approach France positively or not. In part this is related to uncertainty and fearing the unknown. Anything we can do to minimize this, by helping to arrange accommodation for example, is well rewarded academically.

It is clearly also essential to ensure that *assistants* and prospective employees have confidence in their own ability to do what is asked of them. The best contribution we can make to this is by ensuring that they can do their job. In the case of *assistants* this may mean offering them rather meatier and longer courses in ELT than has hitherto been the norm, a skill many recognize they may wish to rely on after graduation. It certainly also means familiarising them in depth with French school conventions, the jargon of the staff-room, the role of staff. Above all it necessitates giving them the time to develop the confidence that they can handle classroom discipline, for example. Here too raising the topic only at the last minute is likely to create more distress than reassurance.

Sentimental attachments, however, whether to ailing parents or prospective spouses, contribute most mightily of all to dissatisfaction and brooding indolence abroad. These may be intractable: it is fairly pointless to order a 20 year old not to fall in love. Nonetheless there is a value in drawing attention to the problem as early as possible in a language student's career. In a sense this encourages them to take responsibility for planning the continuing integration of their own life and studies well before the year abroad begins.

3. The Experience

The year in France is normally spent in one of three ways: as a full-time student, as a language *assistant* or on work-placement. Other arrangements are worth exploring, and it is common for business and some science, law and engineering, students to have periods both of work and of full-time study. In Britain, little research has gone into questioning which of these is more effective or how to maximize the benefits[2].

A recent survey of university French Department "year abroad" requirements and practices suggested that some 34% of language students spend their year as full-time students. (Byram, 1988, 3). (In most institutions the proportion choosing or being required to do so was closer to 25%. A small number of institutions sent more than half of all their students to universities in France.) Changes in the pattern of funding are already ensuring that the costs and benefits of such university study are more closely scrutinised than formerly.

In most cases such study formerly entailed enrolment for first year or DEUG elements of the licence. It is hard to establish how many students nominally enrolled on these courses ultimately sat the examination, but experience suggests that in most institutions this was rare, certainly the exception not the rule. Understandably so, perhaps the non-academic attractions that there were few home institutions willing to offer academic incentives to reward success or enforce sanctions to penalise any but the grossest laxity. This has considerably changed in recent years, and many of the "new" universities already include credits for work done during the year abroad. Former PCFC institutions, responding in this to the CNAA's requirements, also visit all students abroad twice a year, for tutorial as well as supervisory purposes.

The nature of the licence syllabus also meant that many found themselves asked to pursue lengthy lecture courses on much narrower topics than they were accustomed to. Recognition of this by foreign authorities prompted the proliferation of institutes devoted to the provision of courses better adapted to the needs of non-native speakers. Enrolment on such courses guarantees that students will be helped in finding accommodation and obtaining documents, but the cost-penalties are considerable. Likewise perhaps the academic penalties: many now feel that such course should be avoided, for by grouping the learner with other "foreigners" they are precisely defeating the social integration which is one major objective of the year abroad.

Assistantships offer such manifold benefits that it is hard to see why students, when offered choice, so often opt to attend a university instead. Often this seems to be a matter of personality, the more introverted candidates dreading the gregariousness of school life and fearing themselves unable to impose discipline.

Nonetheless, even for those who find that the 12 hours a week they spend in the classroom casts a pall over their free-time, the price may be worth paying. In return they receive a salary, an identity, a place in the community, ready-made associates and potential friends, perhaps also accommodation. They are not merely "just another foreign student". They experience from the inside the wranglings over belated salary transfers, pay rises, strikes, political polemics, personal hostilities that are part of working life. Above all they belong to the kind of institution which has moulded most of the people they meet, an experience without which they can never hope, in any full sense, to speak the same language. All of this they can do within an establishment where, if they wish, they can continue their learning themselves, and where many of their colleagues will be enrolled on courses that too few ofthem seem willing to attend.

There is no doubt that an assistantship enables arts students happily to integrate life, increased insight into French civilisation and language learning. Some other categories of student have always been able to recognize the integral ties between different strands of study - and to complain when they are absent. These are students following vocational degree schemes, who by definition have a clearer awareness than most of their immediate career objectives after graduation. Such students are conscious of the contribution that work-experience can make to their employment prospects. The best are understandably keen to apply their theoretical knowledge of engineering design, marketing techniques or accounting conventions in some real-world context. They already are aware that the culture and language of the work-place are not those of the university.

It is patently desirable in such cases that the overseas should include at least a period of work placement. Under the auspices of ERASMUS, COMETT and other European programmes collaboration between institutions in different countries has greatly facilitated such placements in recent years, not least because the setting-up and supervision of placements is patently easier for those on the spot.

Numerous factors, from the student's personality to prejudices on the part of the home institution, help determine how any given student will spend the year abroad. Desirable scope for individuation exists as much here as elsewhere in the learning process. There is however some evidence that students in work placements show "greater improvement in their command of the spoken language and in their understanding of the associated foreign culture". (Willis et al, 1977, 85) A more recent study by Kloss and Zemke study uses rather different reasoning to argue in favour of the inclusion of a period of work placement in a structured and integrated year abroad. (Kloss And Zemke, 1987, 29)

Unfortunately the immediate interests of the student may no longer be the decisive factor for institutional pressures too have become compelling. Until recently numerous university administrations failed to give a remotely adequate weighting to year-abroad students in their internal allocation of student resources. Some equitable changes have been won thanks to cogent representations from such bodies as the AUPF and a greater consistency now prevails. This in turn, however, has brought closer scrutiny of the content and value of periods spent abroad.

Recent changes in the regulations governing payment of language students' fees have strengthened the administrators' concerns. Under the new funding model universities no longer receive the same income for all students abroad: only half fees are now paid in respect of those students who are in employment and not receiving a maintenance award.

Since any fees payable to overseas institutions are the responsibility of the home university the reasoning behind this may seem clear enough to accountants. The longer term effects are less certain, especially as the value of maintenance awards declines and purely financial considerations drive more students to opt for paid positions. A potential conflict already exists between pedagogic desiderata and the financial self-interest of universities, especially those which have in the past been able to fund overseas study at negligible cost to themselves.

For the institution the financial problem is complex. It may not be beneficial to receive the full fee in respect of a student if all of it has to be spent on paying for enrolment at the British Institute. For the language teacher the clear lesson is the need to stress the role of the year abroad as lynch pin of the degree if funding for it is not to be challenged and the learner's interests undermined.

4. Assessment

One immediate way of achieving this is by locking the year into the assessment scheme more firmly than has happened hitherto. Byram's survey found that only 54% of respondents indicated that their students had to complete written work while abroad. (Byram, 1988, 7). It is not clear in how many of those cases the work contributed significantly to degree assessment. The 1988 position has in any case changed significantly. With the coming modularisation of all courses, where funding will be allocated by student and module, it seems inevitable that the year abroad must become an assessable element of degree schemes, even where (as at Oxbridge) it has not already done so.

Many solutions to the problems of transferable credit-ratings have already been explored in connection with American Junior Year programmes. Possible approaches are also to be found in the numerous "European" degrees run jointly by two or more institutions. An early effect of such collaboration has been the establishment of course units and degree schemes validated by two or more institutions and recognised across national boundaries. Yet again the "newest" universities were exemplary in these fields: where Middlesex led others followed. It may be, however, that such schemes now have more difficulty recruiting British school-leavers than when they were a novelty, and it is noteworthy that many of their most successful participants are French or German.

The primary function of cross-validation was explicitly political: a wish to harmonize professional qualifications, establish equivalences and ensure the mutual recognition of diplomas. It might merely have seemed a consequence of obsessive credentialism. It imposed upon students a layer of assessment that their predecessors had been spared. Despite this, the motivational value of such schemes, incidental though it may be, has been instantly apparent, at least in the enthusiasm with which students compete for places on them. The prospect of accumulating transferable credits contributing to degree-class has proved as compelling as it has long been in equivalent.

It is clear that many students British students enrolled on DEUG courses do not take the relevant examinations. Some do, but it is uncertain whether many of their home institutions have yet developed a formula for integrating such achievement into their final degree assessment[3].

The challenge also remains of finding a similar way of integrating the overseas experience of students following less directly vocational schemes, and those such as assistantships that do not include any element of formal study.

This problem becomes even more acute when students share their time between two different countries and the weight of their assessment must be likewise shared. The most frequent solutions rely on non-library-based researched projects of varying length. These can be used as the subject of oral or viva voce exams on the student's return as a partial answer to colleagues who have misgivings about the work's authorship. As degree class becomes less of a concern, and students take increased responsibility for their own learning, it is likely that "marketable" work produced will be seen as a valuable way of integrating learning and assessment. The Lancaster documentary guide-booklets produced by and for *assistants* under the auspices of the Enterprise Initiative are a good example of this.

Like all Enterprise schemes these required the production of a quasi-commercial output, produced to the specifications of a "client". In this case the CBEVE was kind enough to act as client, and the "product" consisted of local guide-books, written in French, and aimed precisely at the needs and interests of the *assistant*'s successors. Students were invited to identify and provide all of the information about school and locality that they wished they themselves had known prior to their stay. The nature of the documentation sought also obliged them to obtain, by oral enquiry, the views of the pupils and staff on the role and preparation of *assistants*. The product submitted had to be camera-ready copy, which obliged participants to learn French word-processing. This scheme was manifestly motivating to all who participated in it, and produced numerous voluntary and unanticipated benefits, including a video and an introductory commendation from a *préfet*.

Since not all students could be obliged to produce Enterprise projects, these had of course to be assessed in ways strictly comparable to the language projects submitted by their fellows, and made subject to the same *examen oral*. This meant that a copy had to be submitted for assessment and subsequently corrected and proof-read prior to printing. Preliminary results of the scheme suggest that it offered humanities students a valuable way of sharing in the real-world job-satisfaction felt by students in successful business placement. It remains to be seen whether some such scheme can be extended to students on full-time French university courses.

5. *Et après?*

In a sense the year abroad is necessarily integrated into subsequent study upon the student's return merely by virtue of allowing maturer discussion to take place in French. Or so we try to convince ourselves. Yet new ways of working and producing assessments while abroad clearly entail new ways of working and supervising ... not merely on the spot but after the year in France.

It is too easy for the vast amounts of information and understanding garnered in schools and offices to be touched on only in passing: during conversation classes or when briefing the new generation. Students probably spend more time speaking to their friends about their experiences than to their tutors. Yet this is a wealth of current knowledge that those very tutors may not possess. There is a strong case for building upon it, analyzing it, criticizing it, so that the experience itself may be the basis of a new understanding.

This may well imply the creation of new style final year courses. So be it. With many more students starting French more or less ab initio, more splitting the year between two countries, more concerned with non-arts-based subjects, the student population has changed far faster than the courses we offer. We have some cause to be modest about them. Changes in assessment processes and in the very concepts of "student" and "course unit" are upon us. For the mature students of the future, friendships and travel, parental second homes, and telecommunications may well be more potent contributors to their well-being overseas than anything we can offer. It is we who should also be ensuring that these too can be properly integrated into our curriculum, and where appropriate, into assessments of its outcome. Though perhaps students' assessment of the worth of our courses may soon prove more important than our own attempts to assess those very students themselves.

References

Anon, (1988) "Kisses in the Playground", *Times Higher Educational Supplement*, March 1988.

Armstrong, G. (1984) "Life After Study Abroad: A Survey of Undergraduate Academic and Career Choices", *Modern Language Journal*, 68, pp.1-6.

Baron, B and Smith, A (eds.) (1987) *Higher Education in the European Community. Study Abroad in the European Community*, Luxembourg.

Byram, M. (1988) *A Year in France*, University of Durham.

Byram, M. (1992) *The Assistant(e) d'Anglais. Preparing for the Year Abroad.* University of Durham School of Education.

Dalichow, F. and Teichler, U. (1986) *Higher Education in the European Community. Recognition of Study Abroad in the European Community*, Luxembourg.

Evans, C. (1988) *Language People*, Society for Research into Higher Education.

Hantrais, L. (1989) *The Undergraduate's Guide to Studying Languages*, CILT.

Kloss, G. and Zemke, U. (1987) *Foreign Language Competence and Cultural Awareness: Students in European Higher Education exchanges and Work Placements*, Centre for European Studies, University of Manchester/UMIST.

Koester, J. (1986) "A Profile of Foreign Language Majors Who Work, Study and Travel Abroad", *Modern Language Journal*, 70, pp.21-27.

Milleret, M. (1981) "Evaluation and the Summer Language Program abroad", *Modern Language Journal*, 74, pp.483-88.

Nash, D. (1976) "Academic Accomplishment and the Problem of Relevance in an Overseas Studies Program", *Modern Language Journal*, 60, pp.347-352.

Rouxeville, Annie, and Windsor, J. "From Insularity to Integration", in J.A. Coleman and Gabrielle Parker, (eds.) *French and the Enterprise Path*, London, AFLS/CILT, 1992, pp.173-200.

Skutnab-Kangas, T. (1990) "Bicultural Competence and Strategies for Negotiating Ethnic Identity", in Phillipson, R. et al. *Foreign/Second Language Pedagogic Research*, Multilingual Matters.

Strong, M. (1984) "Integrative motivation: Cause and result of Successful Second Language Acquisition", *Language Learning*, 34, pp.1-13.

Willis, F., Doble, G. et al (eds.) (1977) *Residence Abroad and The Student of Modern Languages: A Preliminary Survey*, University of Bradford Modern Languages Centre and School of Studies in Research in Education.

Willis, F (1977) "Absence makes the tongue grow swifter", *Times Higher Educational Supplement*, 12 March 1977.

Notes

1. An SNCF official taking part in discussions on the coordination of Channel Tunnel operations recently dazed his BR counterparts by his reference to two opposing "philosophies ferroviaires".

2. Dyson's study of the language benefits of the year abroad is the major recent British study of the subject. Such research seems commonplace in the USA, perhaps because a shorter period is often involved. (Koestler, 86, 36).

3. Much discussion on the assessment and credit-rating of the year abroad has already taken place, notably within the Standing Conference of Heads of Modern Languages (SCHML).

Integrating Language Learning and Cultural Studies: An Ethnographic Approach to the Year Abroad[1]

Ana Barro and Hanns Grimm, Thames Valley University, London

This chapter draws on the experiences of a research and curriculum development project undertaken over the last three years on a modern languages degree course at TVU. The project, now in its final year, has focused on many current concerns arising from the relationship between language learning and cultural learning. These include a reinterpretation and expansion of the notion of communicative competence to embrace the intercultural dimension.

In order to do this a course has been developed based on the concepts and techniques of anthropology and ethnography, taught over the last two years by lecturers who had no prior training in either of these areas. As those lecturers, we will explain the rationale of the course based on our first-hand knowledge and experiences. Where applicable, we will also refer to student evaluations.

In common with many other HE institutions (cf. Byram, 1988) students on the Applied Language Studies course are required to spend the third year abroad, one semester (4 to 5 months) at a university in each of the countries of their two foreign languages. The students who participated in this project were going to Spain and Germany.

Language degrees in Higher Education frequently concentrate on the technical skills of communicative competence complemented by area studies, where the focus is on content rather than communication. Students also combine language study with other subjects (e.g. a social science, business studies, literature). For students on such undergraduate language courses it is now largely considered a sine qua non that they spend a period abroad in the course of their studies. During their stay abroad the majority of students are expected to produce some kind of written project, dissertation or *mémoire* dealing with an aspect of the foreign society.

Prior to going abroad, students are assumed to have acquired "survival level" linguistic competence. The period of residence abroad is primarily seen as an opportunity for the students to research their projects and to further improve their communicative competence. It is further assumed that this will lead to an increased cultural sensitivity and ability to manage intercultural contacts. There are sound arguments for expecting that immersion in the foreign language and culture will benefit the student in a number of ways.

However, the benefits gained during the period abroad, in terms of increased linguistic competence, understanding of the host society, and the quality of research for the projects, often fall short of expectations, and it is not without reason that there are growing concerns about the value for money of an obligatory period abroad on undergraduate language courses.

These concerns have led the research team to develop an approach to cultural learning which could meet the following objectives:

- to enhance preparation for effective and appropriate cultural learning during the period abroad
- to provide students with systematic training to carry out project work
- to help students integrate better into the host society
- to integrate the year abroad more fully into the curriculum.

Consequently our purpose was to develop a course component which enabled students to shift from largely unconscious cultural learning by immersion in the foreign environment to deliberate and structured learning through reflexive use of field work methodologies which necessitated, and also facilitated, greater participation in the foreign culture. We turned to social anthropology for insights into the methodologies developed for participant observation, ethnographic enquiry and the writing of fieldwork reports. Our approach is based on adaptation of such methodologies to the particular circumstances of the student abroad.

Rationale of the Ethnography Course

It is news to no one that language and culture should be taught in an integrated manner. The model we have chosen is that of the student as ethnographer. Ethnography is the key methodology of anthropology, but is also widely used in teacher education, sociology, linguistics and other disciplines, to get an "insider view" of the culture of a group.

Ethnography is about making sense of the social action of a particular group, in their terms. This involves a detailed description of group members or some aspect of their lives in order to discover the social and cultural patterns of their actions and interactions. It also involves investigating the values, beliefs and assumptions that account for them. (Agar, 1980; Hammersley & Atkinson, 1983; Hammersley, 1992). An ethnography, therefore, involves "thick description" (Geertz, 1975, 6). The ethnographer is constantly collecting rich data around the particular problem that has been foregrounded as an interesting object of study. Such data will involve observation, collection of written documents, formal interviewing and what we have called "ethnographic conversations". These different data sources together resonate in such a way that the ethnographer can read meanings from them. These meanings, in turn, form the basis of further data collection and analysis.

An ethnographic approach is, therefore, holistic in that people's behaviour and the meanings constructed in such behaviour and informing it are always researched in context. In so doing, the ethnographer is attempting to, in Geertz's term "reduce the puzzlement" (1975, 16) that is inevitable when living in a new society. As Hymes has suggested, we are born as ethnographers but somehow lose our capacity to stand apart and reflect on our participation in our cultural practices and those of others (Hymes, 1992).

So, the rationale for training language learners to write ethnographic projects (not to become anthropologists, or even ethnographers) is to equip them with the means to study the detail of particular aspects of these cultural practices, both at home and abroad, to search for the social and cultural patterns which underpin them and so develop their cultural awareness and their communicative competence beyond the exchanging of messages, or simple survival. It is also to enable them to get first-hand knowledge and make sense of their experiences, of what they see and hear, instead of relying exclusively on received wisdom as passed on by teachers, or experts in sociology, economics and so forth.

For our course, we charted a particular and selective path combining social and cultural anthropology and sociolinguistics. We chose ethnography as the most appropriate "lens" for students to use to discover how cultural practices operate.

The ethnography course, then, is both an intellectual and affective preparation for the year abroad. Cultural awareness is developed through detailed participation in and observation of the everyday life and attitudes of ordinary people. While this is usually a part, to a greater or lesser degree, of undergraduate courses, our course aims to equip students with the techniques for eliciting and analysing primary data, with the capacity to draw out and make sense of the cultural meanings embedded in what people say and do.

Through the year abroad learners may acquire an insider's experience of social and cultural practices through interaction. This already fulfils at least one of the requirements of being an ethnographer; to live within the society for an extended period. However, immersion alone does not constitute the ethnographic life. One of the prevailing assumptions in HE language degree courses seems to be that cultural awareness and empathy can be "taught" in the classroom and then "caught" while abroad. We believe more can be done to help students filter their new experiences through reflexive analysis of their own cultural perspectives. Merely leaving this to chance can easily result in those less able to shift their point of view away from stereotypical or superficial notions remaining fundamentally unchanged by their experience or simply not understanding another culture as fully as they might.

The Ethnography Course Programme

The Thames Valley course adopted a two-fold approach, involving on the one hand discussion of key concepts drawn from anthropology and sociolinguistics, and on the other hand, providing opportunities to practice ethnographic methods of data collection, namely field work, participant observation and interviewing (Barro et al. in press).

In planning the course, a major priority has been to achieve a useful balance between the introduction of theoretical concepts and the provision of a "tool kit" of methods (see course outline below). The course begins with students reflecting on their feelings and expectations about the year abroad. In both years, considerable anxiety was expressed, ranging from the practical problems students were likely to encounter, through to more deep-seated fears about losing their identity. The many commentaries concerning culture shock indicate that these fears are to be taken seriously. Indeed, many students who have not had the benefit of systematic preparation never achieve a shift to an insider perspective.

Course outline (Sessions run over a semester, giving a total of 35-40 hours of class contact)

1	What is an ethnographic approach?	8	Participant observation
2	Shared cultural knowledge	9	Interviewing
		10	Data analysis
		11	Social identity and personal boundaries
3	Non-verbal communication and social space	12	Language and identity
4	Family	13	Local level politics
6	Gender relations	14	Belief and action
7	Socialization and education	15	Writing an ethnographic project

---

Most of the conceptual apparatus that is built up in the early sessions is based on the exploration of culture as something shaped and expressed through social interaction. Both primary and secondary socialization are illustrated to see how values, beliefs, roles and relationships are culturally determined and transmitted.

It is a fundamental principle of the course that all the sessions are experiential, as well as intellectually demanding, i.e. based upon students' reflections on their own cultural practices. Thus, students carry out observations and interviews, in public and private places, with strangers and friends, and analyse their findings in class. By carrying out such assignments in a familiar environment students start to question the familiar (to "make strange" in the language of ethnography) and to look for patterns of behaviour.

For example, the week before the session on gender relations, students are asked to observe and listen to a mixed gender conversation. This can be done at home, in class or in the common room. They take notes over a ten minute period, listening in particular for interruptions, variations in loudness, pitch, topic control, use of statements, questions, tag questions etc. They are also asked to observe non-verbal communication. At the beginning of the session, they compare their findings in pairs or small groups and then report back on any patterns detected which could be partly attributable to gender roles. Their findings are then discussed in relation to a text, distributed to the students the week before. In this case the text used "Interaction: The Work Woman Do" (Fishman, 1983), presents a series of observations based on audio material of ten couples in conversation in their homes over a certain period of time. This is then followed up with analysis of video material and class discussion of, for instance, the culturally specific aspects of gender relations, the role of socialization in shaping gender roles, and how these are manifested in the details of very "ordinary" interactions.

At this early stage of the course the focus is less on reaching categorical conclusions, than on drawing concepts out of the raw data, examining the fine-grained details before relating them to the broader picture and encouraging students to pose analytical questions that emerge from the data. This also provides useful training in the techniques of unobtrusive note taking, teasing out description from interpretation, and organizing data.

Because it is from the data that concepts emerge, rather than vice-versa, it is important not to separate concepts, methods and analysis in too rigid a fashion, but rather to fuse them in a dialectic of description and interpretation, as part of a continuing process. Instead of rushing to write up a project based on a predetermined hypothesis, which often results in unreflexive work, students can begin their project investigations as soon as they arrive in the country.

Towards the end of the course students are introduced to more intellectually and methodologically demanding areas, such as the ethnography of communication (looking at speech communities, interactional style, conversation and discourse analysis, speech acts) and what we call Belief and Action which considers the symbolic meaning manifested in the ways people categorise their world views, the relationship between language and power and the rituals of everyday life.

The following extract from one of these sessions will, we hope, illustrate some of the methodologies used.

Integrating Skills and Concepts: A Sample Session

This session offers a more in-depth approach to some of the anthropological material on people and the meanings they construct, exploring the symbolic meanings that underpin social behaviour, such as what people eat and mealtime rituals.

Students are encouraged to think critically and analytically about everyday behaviour, to detect patterns that illuminate symbolic meanings. They also gain further experience of data analysis i.e. making connections between the raw data and broader anthropological concepts.

A subject area such as food lends itself particularly well to analysis of this kind, primarily because it is part of the fabric of our everyday lives, yet is one of the surface realisations of culture that is most readily accessible while abroad. Generally differences are noted not only in the type of food eaten but also different combinations which contravene what we know as "normal". For example, the family mealtimes may be different because they serve a different set of social functions, in different contexts. Food is a topic that most language and area studies courses will cover, as an integral part of culture which is intrinsically interesting. However, this examination is rarely taken further to explore the symbolic interpretations underpinning eating practices. "Food can help create cultural communities and demarcate boundaries, to bind people together or differentiate them." (Lincoln, 1986, 66). Both food and the discourses around food, which embody hierarchies and other socially constructed phenomena, can be a useful starting point for cultural investigation when in the foreign environment.

Observation of cultural practices within "food communities", reveals recurrent elements which are culturally shaped. Adopting a view of culture as a symbolically structured system expressed in terms that Geertz (1975, 10) called "symbolic action", we can begin to distinguish between the functional or "natural" explanations for why we eat or do not eat certain things. Marshall Sahlins'(1990) analysis of the American diet reveals that attitudes toward meat eating can, at a deeper level, be interpreted as a sustained metaphor on cannibalism. According to this analysis pigs and cows are eaten, rather than horses or dogs, for cultural reasons. Horses and dogs are considered more domestic animals, often as pets which can be "part of the family" and therefore not fit to eat. The fact that the French eat horsemeat is often seen as "disgusting" or in some way depraved by American cultural standards. In addition, people distinguish between the innards (tongue, heart, liver) which are considered inferior cuts, and the outer parts, which are further distanced and made more acceptable by using names such as steak. Sahlins makes a further observation that steak is associated with virility, served on special occasions, and is expensive, whereas the cheaper cuts of meat (and, incidentally, "soul food") are associated with lower income groups, who are subtly also characterised as less "civilised". This cannot be explained on the grounds of price or nutritional value. Steak is not more expensive to produce pound for pound but the prices of the meat market are largely influenced by cultural forces of this kind.

This provides an example to students of how the most seemingly trivial "facts" of everyday life can be unpacked to reveal hierarchy, categorisations and symbolic meaning. This is also well illustrated in the article by the British anthropologist, Mary Douglas, called "Taking the Biscuit" (1974) which students were asked to read before the session. This article analyses the highly structured nature of meals and mealtimes within four British working class families. In this instance they are again given an opportunity to find the "strange" and the structured in what appears routine and familiar, as well as again raising issues of description and interpretation.

The pre-session assignment for this session involved interviewing or rather, having "ethnographic conversations" (very informal but focused), with family and friends, concerning their eating habits. Students brought their data to class and were then given half an hour to work in groups on their findings. The aim was, once more, to look for patterns, or contradictions, before presenting them in a diagrammatic form on OHPs to the rest of the group for feedback. Naturally, the groups came up with very different charts and a useful discussion followed not only on their findings but also on the problems of interpreting and categorising information in ways which would make sense to the group. The debate then revolved around the ritualistic components involved and the "natural" versus the cultural explanations. By the end of the session, the whole subject of food was being discussed as an important manifestation of cultural identities, rather than just a case of different nationalities liking or not liking particular foods.

After each session students were asked to complete a diary. One student commented on this session: "One example that was extremely helpful to me was the reason for not eating dogs or human flesh. I wouldn't eat them, but I cannot say that they are harmful. If I do not eat them it is because there are some "laws" that tell me not to do it. But these laws are created by "us". There is not one reality. We create that reality and there are as many realities as different people."

The Period Abroad: Living the Ethnographic Life

Before students go abroad they draw up a detailed project proposal, setting out inter alia the aims of their proposed investigations and how they hope to achieve these aims. They are also required to keep a field diary. The effect is that students start work on their projects and living the ethnographic life immediately, "living it 24 hours a day". As another student said "You just can't get away from it ... ethnography starts coming up all the time".

Integrating the New Experience: Personal Growth

The ethnographic approach provides a powerful integrative focus to their whole experience of living and studying abroad in a foreign environment. Ethnography is not just a methodology serving their projects, but a way of coping with the inevitable culture shock, the "stress-related syndrome whose symptoms can include anxiety, confusion, depression, hostility" (Nolan, 1990, 20). The students who had done the ethnography course were of course not totally immune to this, but had been taught to expect this and to some extent had been able to turn it into a positive learning experience.

Rather than being a source of frustration and irritation the otherness of the new environment was not only seized upon as a source of data, but also enriches their own lives. This is not the excitement of the "honeymoon phase" of the process of "cultural transition", but a constant reflective process of personal adjustment, where students are "redefining" themselves (Nolan ibid.).

Students are well aware of this: "Because I was looking at everyone else's role I couldn't ignore my own. I actually looked at my own position more deeply while I was there in Germany." "You can learn an awful lot about yourself." "You learn a lot through experience in life and this ethnography has been a very big experience for me."

During the year abroad, and we hope, in life generally, students developed further their capacity to adapt to new situations, to cope with the unpredictable, to tolerate ambiguity, and to acquire a more profound grasp of the relationships between language and culture. Comments made by the first cohort of students doing ethnography who have returned for their final year seemed to suggest that these qualities evolved to a significant degree.

The Role Model of the Field Worker

In the knowledge that their projects will have to emerge from data they have accumulated themselves, even fairly shy and normally reticent students have overcome their usual reserve and made things happen. The field worker model provides students with a role that allows and enables them to act differently from what they think is natural to them. Without this focus and methodological support "I never would have had the guts ... if I had not done ethnography. I would probably just have sat there, waiting for people to come to me, or waiting for someone else to introduce me to people, ... as it was I just went up to people. I thought I could never do it, [but] you realize that you have got more confidence than you think."

Observing and Participating: The Outsider Becoming an Insider

Students become very adept at finding out what is happening when nothing seems to be happening. "I really became aware ... it was amazing the sort of things you see when you are looking, that you wouldn't normally notice. You know there is something going on all the time".

Students report that although the negotiation of one's status as insider/outsider can be very challenging at times, and uncomfortable at other times, an appreciation of cultural relativity develops to a considerable degree. As one student commented: "I got much closer to the culture by doing ethnography than I would have done under normal circumstances". This feeling of closeness, of "getting immersed in the place" would suggest not only a greater level of understanding and sensitivity achieved, but also a more critical and reflective attitude to one's own cultural values and standards. It is an experience common to all that one's own ethnocentrism is brought into relief more vividly by being transplanted elsewhere, with no external reinforcements to make one "fit in". So, like the traditional anthropologist, students have been quick to point out the drawbacks, not to say the impossibility of attempting to "go native", and have become more critical both of their own culture and the host culture, as well as more understanding.

It is inherent in this approach that its practitioners inevitably get more involved in everyday life outside the university, by participating more fully in the lives of ordinary people around them, either with host families, or other acquaintances. They have been trained to look to other people, rather than just books and newspapers, for information.

Integrated Language Learning

A natural spin-off of this kind of active and dynamic involvement is a greatly enhanced range of possibilities for developing linguistic skills. The development of active listening is an important part of this process. A few of the comments on this aspect reinforce the idea of increased opportunities to improve communicative competence: "You have to speak to people whereas if you are doing an area studies project you don't have to really, you can just go to a library." "I used my German a lot more than the other students were doing ... I had to use my German more" and "my language improved ... because it made me approach situations differently, it made me more bold where perhaps I wouldn't have been before."

Thus it would seem that ethnography essentially provides the student with a clear purpose for communication, a better idea of what to say and ask, and a way to draw the most value out of everyday encounters.

Shared Cultural Learning and Group Integration

When a number of students are placed at the same foreign institution, the threat of the new and alien environment can easily lead students to construct and maintain their own little England while they are abroad, marking time until they can return home. There is the tendency to "spend most of the time with other English students". The group provides a shield protecting them from the foreign environment, preventing contact with native students, in fact blocking cultural learning and encouraging them to remain outsiders.

We found that even during the preparatory course, the intense experience of learning about themselves and their environment, led in the students' words, to a kind of "bonding". When abroad, rather than looking inwards, students frequently delighted in discovering difference and the support of the group resulted in a heightened experience.

Sharing their experiences, even taking notes for each other when the opportunity arose, meeting regularly to discuss their findings and their projects made them more open and perceptive of different cultural practices, contributing to shared cultural learning.

Integrative Qualities of Ethnographic Project Work

The ethnographic approach to project work facilitates integration in a number of ways. A striking discovery, and one repeatedly stressed by students, is that the attitudes fostered encourage them to get more involved, generally wanting to understand their new environment. They ask more questions, their work even becomes a "topic of conversation" with other students.

Even more important, however, is that they felt they had a reason to look beyond the student community. The particular needs of this kind of project work require students to get "more immersed in the whole place". "I was going out doing things ... you have to go out and look for it."

The Projects

The students carried out their research during the first placement, from October to mid-February. Before going into the field they drew up detailed project proposals which were later adapted to meet the requirements of changing circumstances and situations. From the moment of arrival they cast their nets wide to find a suitable area to investigate. They were already very aware of the need to focus down, although the idea of micro-ethnography is a hard one for students to come to terms with. They initially do not believe they will accumulate enough data by looking at a narrowly delimited area in depth, fearing that they will somehow miss out on the larger picture. To dispel this anxiety, they needed encouragement, as they were not too confident about relying on their own observations, hunches and ideas. In the end they all managed to deal with topics that were very general but with very specific data.

In the first year of the course ethnography was offered to students going to Spain or Germany. Some of the topics chosen are listed below:

- A study of marginality amongst prostitutes in Cadiz
- Gender relations across generations among a group of young people in Seville
- Sevillanas: art or tradition?
- Living in a hall of residence
- Being blind: The relationship between sighted and unsighted
- The classification of foreign students

One student in Seville chose to explore the notion of community and identity amongst a group of friends. His analysis was based on manifestations of rivalry and boundaries. He looked at how his informants defined themselves as outsiders or insiders both in relation to foreigners and also within their own networks of family and friends.

Here, competition emerged as an important theme. By looking at the detail of interactions. The student collected enough data to be able to relate this localised data to the more universal theme of how cultural identity is reinforced and contested.

In this student's case, his research involved close observation of the family he was staying with, and for him, this raised some interesting ethical issues. While the preparatory course had introduced students to some of the potential difficulties of getting too close to informants, he still had to grapple with the sometimes problematic feeling that he was "using" people.

This reflective and challenging process is incorporated into the students' projects, where they document the circumstances of their research, partly as evidence of methodological rigour and partly because the emotional and affective aspects are considered to be an integral factor in the process of doing ethnography.

Thus, the numerous issues that arise from using the ethnographic approach are made explicit. In recognition of this, the criteria used to evaluate the projects include the degree of reflexivity, commitment and initiative shown by the student, in addition to depth of conceptual analysis and use of data.

Conclusion

So far the students who have taken the ethnography course have done so on a voluntary basis, and it would have been expecting too much that this kind of course would answer everybody's needs. There have been students who withdrew from the course; there is some indication that they found the openness and self questioning which the course engenders in class too uncomfortable and preferred to retreat to safer territory.

To quote from student diaries, it tends to "change the way" [students] "look at life in general" and, even though "doing ethnography on yourself" may have "been of great therapeutic help" as one student said, it is not without risks "doing ethnography on your friends". "It can work against you, ... people you ticked along with quite nicely before, all of a sudden you see differently, you start to think, perhaps I don't like you any more."

If it really does "change your life", "being more aware of ... what is going on" and less "opinionated", surely it is a change for the better. Although clearly not everybody wants his or her life changed in this way, it would appear that for the students who have participated in this project the one semester course in the second year has substantially improved the preparation of the students for their time abroad. The course is a bridge between their degree work at home and the year abroad. Thus the year abroad, often considered by some as an extended holiday, is turned into a valuable academic, intellectual, social, and personal experience.

The kind of project work students were engaged in provided an integrative focus for the whole experience. It enabled them to become cultural learners in a broader, more holistic sense. Students discovered for themselves the motivational value of being able to carry out original and independent research. They were also drawing on a conceptual framework and methods clearly based on anthropological, ethnographic and sociolinguistic theories. This is in contrast to many projects, broadly based on area studies, but with no strong conceptual and methodological underpinning.

An additional aspect which we see as beneficial is the integration of academic and informal learning, both during the preparatory course and the year abroad. Parallel to this is the integration of specific skills (e.g. data collection, organisation and analysis of data, eliciting information) and concepts (both sociolinguistic and anthropological). These are transferable skills and ultimately students should be able to apply this kind of approach elsewhere, for instance in the workplace.

There are, still, some issues which remain unresolved. These centre on the ethnographic projects themselves. Despite the enormous additional effort put in by the students in comparison with their peers, the demands of writing ethnographically and in a foreign language meant that the final result did not always do justice to the quality of their fieldwork experiences. There remains also the difficulty of "integration" with colleagues who assess and examine the ethnographic projects. For a linguist without experience of social anthropology and ethnography, it is difficult to use the criteria developed for assessing these projects. However, as the course becomes embedded in the department and more widely known elsewhere, these issues may well be resolved[2].

Apart from these concerns, preliminary findings from the ESRC project, based on conversations, more formal interviews, tutoring, draft and final projects, indicate that the innovation has been largely successful as a process. Students are

- more able to benefit immediately from the early part of the year abroad;

- more critically aware of their own attitudes and behaviour in relation to different cultural experience;

- more able to participate in aspects of life abroad that they would otherwise have ignored;

- able to develop their listening skills and their general observation skills in a systematic and intensive way.

In conclusion, ethnography seems to us a workable as well as an inspirational way of integrating language and cultural learning, an approach by which students can acquire a stronger sense of how these are related in ways that make sense to them, both personally and academically.

References

Agar, M. (1980) *The Professional Stranger*, New York, Academic Press.

Alexander J.C. & Seidman S.(eds.) (1990), *Culture and Society*, Cambridge, Cambridge University Press.

Barro, A., Byram, M., Grimm, H. and Roberts, C. (1992) *BAAL Proceedings, Conference on Language and Culture*, University of Durham, September 1991.

Buttjes D. and Byram M. (eds.) (1989) *Mediating Language and Culture*, Clevedon, Multilingual Matters.

Byram, M. (1988) "A Year in France", (unpublished paper).

Byram, M. (1989) *Cultural Studies in Foreign Language Education*, Clevedon, Multilingual Matters.

Douglas, M. (1974) "Taking the Biscuit", *New Society*, December 19 1974, pp.744-7.

Fishman, P. (1983) "Interaction: The Work Women Do", in Thorne, Kramarae and Henley (eds.), *Language, Gender and Society*, Rowley, Massachusetts, Newbury House.

Furnham, A. and Bochner, S. (1986) *Culture Shock*, London, Methuen.

Geertz, C. (1975) *The Interpretation of Cultures*, London, Hutchinson.

Glaser, B. G. and Strauss, A. L. (1967) *The Discovery of Grounded Theory*, New York, Aldine.

Hammersley, M. and Atkinson, P. (1983) *Ethnography: Principles in Practice*, London, Tavistock.

Hammersley, M. (1992) "Introducing Ethnography." *Sociology Review*, vol. 2, no. 2, pp.18-23.

Hurman, A. (1977) *As Others See Us*, London, Arnold.

Hymes, D. (1992) Remarks made at a Conference on the Ethnography of Communication: Ways of Speaking, Ways of Knowing. Portland State University. August 13-15, Portland, Oregon.

Lincoln, B. (1986) *Discourse and the Construction of Society*.

Nolan, Riall W. (1990) "Culture Shock and Cross-Cultural Adaptation Or, I Was OK Until I Got Here", *Practicing Anthropology*, Vol.12, No.4.

Sahlins, M. (1990) "Food as symbolic code", in J.C. Alexander & S. Seidman (eds.), *Culture and Society*, Cambridge, Cambridge University Press.

Thorne, Kramarae and Henley (eds.) (1983) *Language, Gender and Society*, Rowley, Massachusetts, Newbury House.

Zarate, G. (1989) "The Observation Diary: an ethnographic approach to teacher education", in D. Buttjes and M. Byram (eds.), *Mediating Language and Culture*, Clevedon, Multilingual Matters.

Notes

1. The material findings in this article are the preliminary results of an ESRC funded project on Cultural Studies In Advanced Language Learning in which the authors are taking part. The project is directed by Celia Roberts, Reader in Language Studies at Thames Valley University, and Mike Byram, Reader in Education at Durham University.

2. Course materials will be available by the end of 1993.

Language Learning: Developing Autonomy

Marie-Christine Press, University of Westminster

1. Introduction

The last ten years or so have seen an unprecedented surge in the demand forlanguage tuition, as exemplified in Higher Education by the development of new courses, and new modes of delivery, such as the Open University French language modules available from 1994, or the University of London BA Degrees in European Languages for External Students. While stressing the self-discipline and drive necessary for learners to achieve their goals, such programmes offer flexible and exciting alternatives to traditional courses. At the same time, new forms of learning are also being explored and made available through language centres attached to, or independent from language departments. University language centres have been developing their own research and training programmes into alternative modes of language learning - open learning, self access, independent study[1].

The traditional providers of education are thus manifesting renewed interest in forms of learning which have, after all, been in existence since Antiquity. The autonomous learner, the autodidact, is not a new phenomenon. What *is* new is the focus on the concept of learner autonomy which has been characteristic of much educational research lately. True, there is some concern that this fashionable concept might be used rather indiscriminately. However, very few people today need convincing of the positive, enhancing effects of handing over to students greater responsibility for their own learning. Not because it is cheaper, or more convenient. But because there is strong evidence that helping learners towards greater autonomy will help them learn better. It also provides teaching institutions with an opportunity to reassess their traditional courses, to integrate learning systems which allow greater flexibility and variety in the light of current educational thinking, and of students' expectations.

This article looks at ways in which the concept of learner autonomy has been developed and applied to language learning, and explores its integration to traditional language courses. First, a short survey of the background to current research in learner autonomy will point to some familiar, but important themes: student-centred learning, and authentic tasks. Then we shall see how the concept of autonomy applies to the language learner, specifically the adult learner who wishes to learn in a principled way. Different programmes which support autonomous learning will be described to illustrate the value of learner training and its implications. Finally, traditional classroom methodology will be reassessed in the context of an institution wishing to offer its students the educational benefits of greater self-direction.

2. Background to the Concept of Learner Autonomy

Broadly speaking one can identify three main currents which have overlapped and combined to offer a more holistic view of learning, and language learning in particular. These are the educational concerns of the post-war period, the cognitive revolution in psychology, and developments in theories of second and foreign language acquisition[2].

The educational literature mentions studies in the States in the sixties, which first started looking in some detail at adult learners and their participation in self-directed educational activities. A parallel shift was taking place in language acquisition research. Through classroom observation, researchers were trying to establish the advantages of one language teaching method over another. There, observation moved from teachers and their faithful adherence to prescriptive teaching methods, to descriptive classroom interaction, thus emphasising the centrality of the *learning* processes. At the same time, developments in educational psychology highlighted the *individual* aspects of personality and cognitive style, and created an interest in learner strategies in second language learning. More systematic research in the seventies established that self-directed adult learners are organised around a "learning project". In other words, they make conscious decisions about what they learn, why, how and when, and about outcomes. This is a path which thousands of Open University students have followed for the last thirty years.

Such concepts are clearly relevant to second and foreign language learning where the variety of needs and opportunities for language use are literally endless: because of the infinite nature of the task it is particularly important that learners should have an awareness of their goals and learning outcomes. Furthermore this view fits closely with the communicative view of language. Both have had a combined impact on language teaching methodology: after the rigid language drills and teaching methods of the fifties and sixties, there has been an increased awareness of the need for learners to continue learning on their own well after instruction had taken place. It is believed that this is more likely to happen successfully in a learner-centred environment where learners

- are presented with real-life problems, relevant to their knowledge, interests and needs
- are given responsiblility for their own learning, through a definition of their learning project
- are given the tools, or skills, necessary for learning, through study skills and learner training.

Responsibility for one's own learning is at the core of the notion of learner autonomy, as will be seen when looking at the definitions which have been given of the concept.

3. Defining Autonomy in Language Learning Schemes

At the forefront of research in second language learning, learner strategies and learner autonomy, a few institutions have created pioneering systems and applications which have set important parameters for further reflection and developments. One such institution is the Centre de Recherches et d'Applications Pédagogiques en Langues (CRAPEL) of the Université de Nancy II. Their definition of autonomy is of interest. Henri Holec, Philip Riley, Harvey Moulden and others at the CRAPEL see autonomy both as an attitude, and as an aim.

- an *attitude* on the part of the students who will be encouraged away from a position of consumers of learning programmes, towards that of producers of their own learning programmes, or at the very least - as Harvey Moulden put it: "des consommateurs avertis" - informed, mature consumers.
- an *educational* aim, one which our educational system must foster. Autonomy implies then a redefinition of the respective roles of teacher and learner. It implies handing over responsibility (but not imposing it). In this

light, we are reminded that teaching does not cause, but helps learning.

When looking at strategies used by language learners, Anita Wenden (1987) states that educational theorists have developed a set of assumptions about adult learners' needs. The assumptions are of two kinds:

3.1. Adult learners conceive of themselves as self-directing personalities. This assumption for instance inspired the psychologist Curran (1976) to develop a "counselling-learning" approach to FL learning, through which the learner progresses from dependence on the teacher to self-sufficiency. And the 1980s saw a proliferation of learner guides encouraging self reliance on the part of the learner - not to say they didn't exist before, viz. E.Nida (1957) *Learning a Foreign Language: a Handbook Prepared Especially for Missionaries*! One of the latest examples of this "whole person" approach is the new BBC language course *Italianissimo*, in which the author describes the central concept of learner autonomy around which the material is organised. It is articulated around key themes: flexible learning, personal objectives, learning strategies, achievement targets. It rests on the assumption that giving students the tools of language learning has to do with raising their awareness of the process. In this light it might be worth considering the second set of assumptions which Anita Wenden describes:

3.2. Some "de-conditioning" must take place before adults can realise their power, and their full potential. Critical reflection on the part of the learner is imperative. Entrenched assumptions and attitudes about learning and language have to be challenged[3]. Anita Wenden goes so far as to argue that a reliance on learning techniques and learner training may be doomed to failure, or at any rate be of limited effectiveness, unless accompanied by an internal change of consciousness, a "self deconditioning".

How can the aim, and the attitude of autonomy be translated in the context of higher education, from the point of view of the language lecturer, and that of the language student? Answers to the issues of control and choice will vary according to the goals of the institution, the timing and mode of course delivery, methods of assessment and support, learning resources ... Observation and investigation have shown that many students learning a language or languages as a major or minor part of a Degree course would welcome, and benefit from an element of self direction for some of the following reasons:

- the pace of a given course is too fast or too slow
- the group is of mixed ability
- the topics in the syllabus meet the students' needs or expectations only partially
- they prefer working in their own way
- they cannot in fact attend all classes.

This last case is likely to become increasingly widespread as mature and impoverished students need to take part-time paid work in order to support themselves. Increasing learner autonomy will mean giving the student more say in some of these areas. But it must also be stressed that learner autonomy does not mean the absence of a teacher. It cannot be limited to learning without a teacher, nor is it synonymous with self access.

4. Learner Autonomy: Applications

Learner autonomy implies that learners know how to learn. As suggested earlier, the autonomous learner will know not only what to learn, but why, how, when, where, and to what end. Furthermore, learners come to a L2 with a great deal of knowledge about language and communication. If, as we believe, students learn better when all of their resources are tapped, it follows that teaching should offer an element of consciousness raising, or learner training in the cognitive, the affective as well as the procedural domains. Learner training will aim to help learners clarify and assess their beliefs, expand their repertoire of learning strategies, and learn how to regulate their learning by defining their objectives, choosing materials, and evaluating outcomes.

4.1. Learning How To Learn a Language

Three examples will be used to illustrate how the notion of autonomy can be developed and integrated to traditional foreign language courses. In the first example, Odile Régent and lecturers from the CRAPEL approach the issue by exploring with language students two aspects of language learning strategies. The sessions are part and parcel of a course of EFL in the context of a "Languages for All" policy. The second example describes a resource created for self directed study, while the third shows a "learning to learn" programme integrated to a general study skills programme for language students. It is worth noting that a distinction between learning (or metacognitive) strategies, and communication (or cognitive) strategies will be used here to clarify the process[4].

4.1.1. Metacognitive strategies involve awareness of learning, and managing information:

- thinking about the learning process, and more specifically about the nature of language learning. For example: learning rules by rote, but also being able to generate rules.
- planning for learning, e.g. defining needs and objectives, being aware of learning styles, and the role of memory.
 - monitoring of learning while it is taking place, e.g. in oral communication, concern with correctness, pronunciation.
- self evaluation of learning after the learning has taken place, e.g. usefulness of errors as a sign of hypothesis testing and growing autonomy.

4.1.2. Cognitive strategies involve awareness of language, manipulation or transformation of the material to be learnt:

- ability to use compensation strategies, e.g. by asking for repetition or clarification, looking puzzled ...
- use of comprehension strategies when listening and reading, e.g. by attending selectively to meaning and form ...
- awareness of audience, register, intention, cultural implications.
- awareness of the characteristics of oral and written discourse, e.g. cohesion, coherence ...

Example 1: Learner Training

A 30-hour programme of learner training was designed by Odile Régent for around 600 first-year Science students at Nancy University. In an account of this pilot scheme (Régent, 1989), she argues that instead of the usual 30 hours of EFL being taught to large, heterogeneous groups two hours a week, the teacher's and the students' time and expertise are better used if each session is devoted to a particular aspect of "learning how to learn", while tasks in the English language are performed by the students in their own time. The programme covers training in listening comprehension (8 hours), reading comprehension (8 hours), and self-directed study in the form of an individual -or group project (14 hours). Both the listening and the reading comprehension programmes introduce students to

- language characteristics - in their case scientific written discourse; specialised lexis; how information is organised around factual, communicative, pragmatic, cultural features ...
- specific learning techniques, such as using previous knowledge to make hypotheses; anticipating; using questions to generate or check meaning, using a dictionary, a script ...
- hands-on experimentation in class: applying appropriate techniques to selected texts and evaluating results.

Progress in listening and reading comprehension is formally assessed, usually with a multiple choice questionnaire on a long text.

The self-directed study element encourages a change of attitude in students, towards greater self direction. It involves a preliminary brainstorming session in sub-groups, so that projects can be defined and sources of support explored (libraries, self access centre, radio and TV, clubs ...). When the projects are under way, students book tutorials to discuss work in progress. On completion of their projects, they present a final oral report covering objectives, sources and materials used, work techniques, time spent and monitoring of progress. Assessment of the project is based on the final report, and it is "collaborative", i.e. a mark is discussed and agreed between the teacher and the student.

Example 2: Listening Comprehension and Independent Study

An example of a training programme in one specific domain is the CRAPEL *Listen for Yourself* guide to listening without a teacher (Bowden and Moulden, 1989). Self direction is an important feature of the learner training course for Nancy University M.I.A.Ge (computer applications in business management) students (See Duda, Moulden & Rees, 1988). The listening guide is intended for students working on their own and wishing to improve their aural skills. It suggests 36 different ways of using a recording, and it covers all eventualities (including not finding a diagnosis for your own specific problem - in which case you are urged to complain to the author - a worthwhile exercise in autonomy for any student!) It addresses the issues of

- different listening modes: gist / detailed / selective, and how to make progress by clarifying objectives and using techniques appropriate to different listening modes;
- how to choose recordings, according to criteria of one's objectives and level, and the availability of a transcript;

- listening strategies for gist and detailed comprehension - this is demonstrated via written texts, and the reader is encouraged to use similar techniques relevant to real-time listening: concentrating on what is known, using contextual clues, sentence structure, voice tone, guessing what might have been said ...
- accurate diagnosis of listening problems, for example: confusing similar words or sounds, losing the thread because of one word, problems with aural discrimination or segmentation, or remembering what has just been said, missing
connections, not discerning the general structure of the text ...
- ways of improving aural comprehension. A techniques bank helps the listener in two complementary directions: working on the problems, and practising the target skills of gist listening, listening for detail, and selective listening. Advice includes: reading the transcription of a recording before listening to check unknown words and phrases, leaving one free to concentrate on the way they are pronounced; checking comprehension or memory of specific words (e.g. connectors) by creating one's own gapped transcripts; stopping a recording from time to time to predict what comes next; increasing memory by starting with very short texts, then progressively longer ones ...
- appraising one's work: a critical attitude to one's progress is encouraged, instead of passively waiting for improvements to occur. The authors stress the importance of planning the task, keeping a record of each step, and systematic revision. One could usefully combine the use of a CALL programme with the transcript of a recording to produce various exercises supporting revision and reinforcement.

Example 3: Study Skills for Language Learners in Higher Education.

This Foundation module is offered to first-year students at the University of Westminster in the first semester of their Modern Languages Degree. The aim is to raise students' awareness of their own skills, both in the metacognitive and the cognitive domains, and to offer them systematic learner training and practice in different strategies. The programme fits a two-hour weekly session spread over twelve weeks and covers general *study* skills in parallel with more specific *language learning* skills:

Study skills:	Language learning skills:
- Learning styles: learning efficiently	- What "good language learners" do

- Time management	- Prioritising/Little and often/Revision
- Organisation/ Memory	- Mnemonics/ using native language/ organising vocabulary
- Using reference material/ the library and other resources	- Dictionaries/Grammars/self access language centre
- reading/note-taking	- Reading in F.L.
- Listening/note-taking	- Listening in F.L.
- Writing essays	- Writing in F.L.
- Oral presentations	- Speaking in F.L.
- Monitoring progress/Self and peer assessment	- Cultural awareness

At the beginning of the course the students reflect on their attitude to learning and fill in a questionnaire which assesses their degree of self directedness and motivation. The same questionnaire is used again in the last session of the programme, and students usually note an encouraging movement towards greater autonomy. During the course of the programme they reflect on their learning experience by writing regular diary entries which will form part of the final module assessment - other criteria being attendance and participation in the various activities. Those include practice in formulating personal objectives in self directed language study, by writing a learning contract and a plan of work for a specific period of time.The students are also encouraged to reflect on ways in which to use available facilities such as the self access centre, and how this can help them develop new, more confident and independent learning patterns. A typical task in the self access language centre might be listening comprehension. Suggested techniques will include many of the ideas offered in the previous two examples. Another area of learner training is self monitoring, which would include learning to keep a logbook of work done, looking for self-correcting exercises (CALL or other sources), etc. But it is clear that such activities will be considered worthwhile by the students only insofar as they are integrated with their language programme, and adequately supported through appropriate advice and monitoring from the teacher.

4.2. Learner Support

When learner autonomy becomes a clearly identified institutional aim, the issue of learner support has to be addressed as a priority - on a par with the availability of materials. It needs to be fully integrated with the student's learning. Experience shows that even if a self access facility provides the most flexible form of access to a good range of materials, it will only meet learners' demands if

- students and teachers are trained in its uses
- students are encouraged by their teachers to use a variety of materials with which the teachers are themselves familiar
- students are encouraged to work together as well as individually
- teachers adopt a more "counselling" role and help students monitor their progress, for instance by discussing and negociating assessment criteria.

Not only do new arrivals need to be introduced to the facilities of a self access language centre - and of a library and a computer centre. It is also crucial that teachers demonstrate their faith in the students' ability for self study! Careful integration throughout the course of language tasks completed in the self access language centre and including an element of formal assessment, contributes to a positive perception of self access and a development of autonomy among students.

These requirements can be met through training in groups. Or they may be met through helping and tutoring individuals, sometimes in a remedial context. For instance a tutoring session can help a student

- diagnose specific needs or problems
- define personal objectives
- agree a contract of work for a given period of time
- select appropriate tasks, materials and strategies for language work
- choose appropriate forms of assessment
- keep a record of work done, progress achieved, problems encountered
- review/revise original objectives, and so on.

It will be clear that in this context, we are not talking about a student simply acquiring language skills. We are talking about personal development, and the development of autonomy.

4.3. Value of Learner Training

Some researchers stress the culturally-bound nature of learner strategies, others their psycho-affective dimension. Take for example the avoidance of translation: it is usually considered a desirable strategy in language learning. However it is pointed out that it may be an especially difficult technique to develop for a strongly ethnocentric learner, who for psycho-affective reasons needs to remain closely connected to his or her first language. In order not to lose sight of the overall aim of learner training - which is to develop learner autonomy, caution is therefore advocated when recommending specific strategies and training students in their use.

It must also be noted that learner strategies which are useful in a classroom situation may need to be modified in a different context. This is common sense. If we consider the above examples of learner training, it is clear that the self-directed study element of the programmes is a crucial ingredient. It aims to encourage students to apply for themselves and according to their own needs some of the strategies presented and explored in class. Perhaps more importantly it gives them an opportunity to define their own priorities through a project (see below), to choose appropriate means of achieving their goals, and generally to adopt a critical attitude towards their learning.

In any case, learner training should consider issues such as the appropriateness of the strategy to the task, the explicitness of instructions, the integration of the training with language learning activities and to some extent the level of learner maturity. By combining the expertise of the teacher-tutor with the skills which the student brings to the learning task, one hopes to come closer to the the desired aim of greater self direction on the part of the learner.

5. Learner Autonomy and Classroom Methodology

This section and the next seek to highlight further ways in which the concept of autonomy can enhance language learning in a fairly traditional setting. Dickinson (1987, pp. 36 ff.) offers a helpful overview of the major tasks of the language teacher in the classroom, from pedagogical planning to teaching and assessment, not forgetting management and organisational tasks, counselling and supporting. He then considers ways in which the learner can in fact be encouraged to take on some of those tasks. By taking more part in the setting and the process of their learning, students are helped to view the learning experience as a joint responsibility. Furthermore, the application of some of the values of autonomy in a group context will go a long way towards meeting the criticisms of those who have sensed that the concept of autonomy in learner training has been abused somewhat - through neglect of the social dimension of learning in general and of language learning in particular[5].

Activities which promote autonomy include the following, and more (once again, it is only for clarity that I use the distinction between learning and management tasks):

5.1. Language Learning Activities:

- Practice, typically through role playing and simulation, in initiating discourse, responding, and all the usual features of authentic, meaningful oral, e.g. a summer job interview, or a telephone call to a difficult landlord, or returning overdue books to the College library ...
- In the same light, project work fosters communication of content through practice of the four skills in context. For example a group of students write and perform their own TV broadcast - news, current affairs, a debate ... after carrying out appropriate research. They can video their own performance for practice, or as a record to be kept for themselves or for other students in a self access video library.
- Extensive reading or listening, which can be done outside class time, can be followed by description and group discussion of techniques used. It can be done by a group of students around topics selected by themselves: they will then present a report to the class both on the content and group methods used.
- Trouble-shooting and peer support: checking corrections on written work and discussing with peers ways of avoiding errors or improving style; spending five minutes at the end of each class to note down the one or two most salient things learnt, and any points that still need attention and practice. This can lead to students asking to be tested formally on specific items. This overlaps with:

5.2. Management Activities:

- Collaborative decision making: defining long and short term objectives; drawing up a class work contract outlining the responsibilities of teacher and students; choosing activities and materials, as above or, in less advanced language contexts, selecting activities at different levels of ability - E.g. reading tasks with several degrees of support, with or without questions ...; preparing questions on a text for other students to answer.
- Self- and peer-monitoring, assessment and support, for example through

students keeping their own grammar checklist of most frequent mistakes; proof-reading each other's work, e.g. in the context of producing a class news magazine, or a review of current affairs to be circulated to the whole group/year/department ... regular information exchange on cultural events, and on all available resources: libraries, local native speakers, cultural centres; planning group activities in the self access centre ...

Nothing very new is being proposed here: good language classroom teaching displays some or many of the features described above. The extent to which learners can exercise learning and management choices will give a fair idea of how much autonomy is a feature of our classroom practice. Through such activities students are encouraged to utilise their whole personality: rationality, capacity for analysis, judgement, emotions. In short they are more self directed. However, self monitoring and self assessment are often neglected, or even resisted by teachers and students alike. And yet the ability to evaluate one's own work is a skill which graduates have been shown to rate very highly[6].

6. Learner Autonomy and Assessment

As has already been indicated, assessment is effectively present from the start of a learning project. It goes hand-in-hand with every aspect of planning and monitoring that the learner is engaged in, from the initial assessment of personal needs and objectives up until the final, summative assessment which usually forms part of an academic course. In one sense, strictly "autonomous" learners would not need to submit themselves to external evaluation of their performance (although clearly they would retain the choice to do just that). However, we are dealing mostly with students who have chosen to enrol on taught, examined and accredited language courses, and whom, for pedagogic and broadly educational and social reasons, we hope at the same time to help become truly autonomous, i.e. who will know how to learn and be able to take charge of their learning.

6.1. Norm-referenced Assessment vs. Criterion-referenced Assessment

In our experience, students assessed in the traditional manner tend to show a certain disinterest for the feedback we give them. Generally we regret this state of affairs, but we accept it. We may feel uneasy about perpetuating an attitude of dependence on marks. But we may also feel that little can be done about it in a system which rests on norm-referenced, external assessment. Norm-referenced criteria encourage ranking in order of "good" to "poor" with little explicit reference to what constitutes a good, or an unsatisfactory performance. If the institution does not provide clear criteria, students find it harder to reflect on their own performance and to form their own, internalised view of what a good, or a poor performance is.

But there has been a change in attitude and expectations in the last few years: for one thing, students having embarked on increasingly costly studies now want to know what, and how, they are going to be taught, and how they are going to be assessed. There are still relatively few language courses in higher education which refer explicitly to assessment criteria, for instance in the form of graded objectives. However, it will be noted that this is also changing, for a variety of reasons which may include the impact of the National Curriculum, and increased contacts (and competition?) with other language providers. It will therefore be in our interest as well as in the interest of our students' education to look more closely at the related issues of criterion-referenced teaching, self assessment and autonomy.

6.2. Self Assessment

"Self assessment involves students taking responsibility for monitoring and making judgements about aspects of their own learning. It requires of them
- to think critically about what they are learning
- to identify appropriate standards of performance
- to apply those to their own work." (Boud, 1986)

A number of studies, experiments and reports point to the benefits of even a small measure of self assessment in the most traditional classroom setting. Practical applications include learner diaries, self assessment charts, and long-term language projects which combine all the stages of a fully self-directed programme of study (Boud, 1986; Moulden, 1990; Oskarsson, 1980).

6.2.1. Learner Diaries

More to do with self-monitoring than with strict assessment, a diary encourages students to take a critical look at their learning activities. Noting from day to day or week to week what has been done, how, with what measure of success, difficulty or enjoyment, can be a powerful help in the process of "owning" one's learning. It should also enable the learners from time to time to take stock of how successful their use of specific learning strategies has been, with a view to trying different ones. A diary can also be a helpful link between the learners and their tutors.

Example: **Diary Notes** (Self access language centre, University of Westminster). A pro forma diary invites learners to keep a detailed record of each work session.

DIARY NOTES

DATE:
TIME SPENT:
ACTIVITY:

LISTENING/READING/SPEAKING/WRITING/GRAMMAR/VOCABULARY

TITLE OF DOCUMENT USED and Page/Counter n° ref.:

WHAT I LEARNED AND HOW I PRACTISED:

WHAT DIFFICULTIES I HAD/STILL HAVE:

WHAT I INTEND TO DO NEXT:
- REVIEW
- TEST
- ASK FOR EXPLANATION
- ....

6.2.2. Assessment Charts

Self assessment charts can be found for instance in G. Ellis & B. Sinclair (1989). They have generously waived copyright for class use of those charts at the end of the book. A chart can provide a useful incentive to learners, particularly if they have been given the opportunity to assess their aptitude at the beginning of a course, e.g. a diagnostic test, or a performance profile. It will suggest to them that they are in a position to decide how well they are doing - but in relation to what? There again criteria will have to be made very explicit - e.g.

- what is expected of them in reading/listening comprehension (and of what kind of source text);

- whether grammatical accuracy is expected, and in what areas;
- what speaking or writing skills are consistent with their level (and again in what mode, and with a premium on fluency or accuracy);
- the place given to cultural awareness, etc.

6.2.3. Language Projects

A further step along the road to autonomy will be accomplished if students are given the opportunity of devising their own objectives: they can then decide which aspects they need to practise and test. This is indeed the approach favoured by Harvey Moulden of the CRAPEL. (See Moulden 1990, pp. 107-19) Students are asked to design their own language learning projects, by following a careful process of choosing a situation and a field of language use, carrying out a diagnosis of their difficulties in the given area, and selecting appropriate material and tasks. Curiously in this instance, assessment of the project appears to be done mostly by the teacher, although it is based on the students' diaries and own accounts of how they handled the task. In this respect, Odile Régent's collaborative (i.e. student with teacher) evaluation of very similar students' projects, as mentioned earlier in this article, (Régent, 1989) seems to reflect more closely the philosophy of learner autonomy.

We have seen how, for learners to become truly autonomous, they should be given at least some say in the decision-making process, from the initial decision to learn for a specific goal, to what has to be learnt in order to achieve it, to how and when and in what order to learn it, to evaluating outcomes - in short they should be able to "manage" learning. It is this last stage in the process - self assessment, and evaluating learning outcomes, which students and institutions will need to integrate, and learn to manage.

7. Conclusion

Language teachers have been presented with new challenges, and expectations of flexibility and transferability linked with new socio-economic and cultural factors. Educational research has supported new methodologies which have contributed to the development of the notion of learner autonomy and its integration, aided by technological advances, in the context of language learning and teaching. It has been possible, no doubt because of the high correlation which exists between on the one hand the communicative methodology resulting from theories of language and language acquisition, and on the other models offered by cognitive, psychological and social sciences, which underpin the overall educational aims and values realised in learner autonomy.

Given the new contexts in which these developments have been taking place - often away from the classroom and into the video library, the resources centre, the self access centre and other places, it is becoming important to set up methods and procedures of self monitoring and assessment which will reflect adequately the new significance being given to learner autonomy.

References

Allwright, D. (1984) "Why Don't Learners Learn What Teachers Teach - the Interaction Hypothesis". In Singleton, D. and Little, D., eds., *Language Learning in Formal and Informal Contexts*, Dublin, IRAAL.

Allwright, D. and Bailey, K.M. (1991) *Focus on the Language Classroom*, Cambridge University Press.

Arthur, L. (1990) *Independent Study among Foreign Language Learners*. Unpublished Report, Department of Adult and Community Studies, Goldsmiths' College, University of London.

Boud, D. (1986) *Implementing Student Self Assessment*, Green Guides N° 5, Higher Education Research and Development Society of Australasia.

Bowden, J. and Moulden, H. (1989) "'Listen for Yourself': a small handbook for improving aural comprehension of English without a teacher", *Mélanges Pédagogiques*, CRAPEL, pp.19-29.

Dickinson, L. (1987) *Self Instruction in Language Learning*, Cambridge University Press.

Dickinson, L. (1992) *Learner Autonomy 2 : Learner training for language learning*, Dublin, Authentik.

Duda, R. and Riley, P. (1990) *Learning Styles*, Presses Universitaires de Nancy.

Ellis, G. and Sinclair, B. (1989) *Learning to learn English*, Cambridge University Press.

Gathercole, I. (ed.) (1990) *Autonomy in Language Learning*, CILT.

Holec, H. (1987) "The Learner as Manager: Managing Learning or Managing to Learn?", in A. Wenden and J. Rubin (eds) *Learner Strategies in Language Learning*, Prentice Hall International.

Holec, H. (1988) *Autonomy and self-directed learning: present fields of application*, Strasbourg, Council of Europe.

Little, D. (1989) *Self-access Systems for Language Learning*, Authentik in association with CILT.

Little, D. (1991) *Learner Autonomy 1: Definitions, Issues and Problems*, Dublin, Authentik.

Moulden, H. (1990) "Assessing the self-directedness of foreign language learners", *Mélanges Pédagogiques*, CRAPEL, pp.107-19.

Narcy, J.-C. (1991) *Comment mieux apprendre l'anglais*, Les Editions d'Organisation.

Oskarsson, M. (1980) *Approaches to Self-assessment in Foreign Language Learning*, Pergamon Press.

Régent, O. (1989) "Apprendre à apprendre en grand groupe", *Mélanges Pédagogiques*, CRAPEL, pp.41-9.

Richardson, V. (1992) "Learner Training", *Modern English Teacher*, Vol 1, N°1, pp.42-3.

Riley, P. (1990) "Learners' representations of language and language learning", *Mélanges Pédagogiques*, CRAPEL, pp.65-7.

Sheerin, S. (1989) *Self-Access*, Oxford University Press.

Skehan, P. (1989) *Individual Differences in Second-Language Learning*, Edward Arnold.

Tremblay, N.A. (1986) *Apprendre en situation d'autodidaxie*, Les Presses de l'Université de Montréal.

Wenden, A. and Rubin, J. (1987) *Learner Strategies in Language Learning*, Prentice Hall International.

Willems, G.M. and Riley, P. (eds.) (1989) *Foreign Language Learning and Teaching in Europe*, Amsterdam, Bureau Lerarenopleiding & Free University Press.

Willing, K. (1989) *Teaching how to Learn*, N.C.E.L.T.R. Macquarie University, Sydney.

Notes

1. For example a two-day conference at the Language Centre of the University of Cambridge in association with CILT, on the adult language learner and self-access (13-15 December 1992).

2. See Susan Sheerin's "State of the Art" article on Self-access, in the July 1991 issue of *Language Teaching Abstracts* (CUP). It offers a useful overview of recent historical developments in foreign language teaching, as well as several examples of self-access facilities in various settings.

3. The point can be illustrated by some interesting results of a questionnaire on Independent Study among FL Learners. It was administered in November 1990 to 410 evening language learners in the Department of Adult and Community Studies, Goldsmiths' College, University of London. Among the respondents, 45% of women and 53% of men said they would prefer learning a FL in a one-to-one situation, i.e. with an individual tutor. But when asked: "Who or what keeps you *motivated*?", 54% of beginners and intermediate, and 62% of advanced learners said: "the tutor", but 76% of the former and 60% of the latter said: "achievement". They also showed a healthy ability to work for themselves: 61% declared studying in addition to set homework, and spending 3 to 4 hours a week on independent study.

4. But see K. Willing (1989, 144-5): "Given that many of the cognitive operations which need to be performed in a conversation, for example, inevitably require the assimilation of new data with an existing knowledge base, clearly an important learning function is necessarily occurring. In this sense many communication strategies may be seen as necessarily incorporating strategies of learning. Therefore, for practical purposes in the language teaching context, a sharp distinction between these two notions would not in fact be useful."

5. Vic Richardson (1992) argues that learner training has tended to isolate students by encouraging them to work by themselves, thus depriving them of the benefits of group dynamics and leading to a loss of motivation.

6. In a major survey of graduates of the University of New South Wales (Boud, 1986), respondents rated the ability to evaluate their own work second only to "solving problems". "But only 20% of graduates felt that the contribution of the university to the achievement of this goal was 'considerable', while 27% thought the university's contribution to it was 'little'".

An Integrated Approach to the Teaching of Literature on a European Languages and Business Course

Margaret Parry, Leeds Business School
(Leeds Metropolitan University)

Experience has shown that whilst students are frequently attracted to an applied languages degree because it does not require them to study literature, by the end of the first year a substantial number of them are having a change of heart. Languages purely allied to the study of business and the socio-economic and political context of the country -or countries- concerned does not always provide the more personal satisfaction and enjoyment they crave, whether one associates the idea of satisfaction with the exploration of more fundamental human and psychological issues than those normally intrinsic to the study of business, at least in its early stages, or with the linguistic enjoyment and stimulation which come from exposure to language deployed in its richest, most imaginative forms. It was with such students in mind that it was decided at Leeds to offer a second-year option module on the French and their working environment. The specific title given to the module, so as to emphasize its relevance to a core business module programmed in the previous semester, was "People in Organisations; case studies from French Literature".

The module was taught entirely in French. It lasted for one semester and was allocated two hours of class contact per week, taught in a single block, supplemented by four hours of private study, this ratio determined by the need to allow students adequate reading and preparation time for the weekly seminars. Sixteen students enrolled for the module, which was one of ten options offered in the course's first year of operation.

In broad educational terms, the course aimed to make students think critically and creatively about the working environment, about the concepts of hierarchy and subordination, enterprise and the enterprise culture, public competition and private integrity. It raised questions about relationships of class and minorities, about personal fulfilment and group solidarity, about career choices and their implications. In short, the aim was to contribute to the development of a reflective, mature worker, conscious of the complexity of forces which define one's working situation, and capable of making the right sort of choices and decisions and value judgments in relation to that situation.

As regards the literary and linguistic objectives of the course, it sought to encourage students not only to read and to enjoy reading, but also to develop their sensitivity to the linguistic variety and expressive range of literary-based writing, as compared with the functional, uniformized language of the standard business text. It was hoped that the students' own expressive and communicative powers would be enriched in the process. A further consideration was the cultural phenomenon, perhaps particular to France by virtue of its educational system, of the literary/humanist outlook which typifies so many business specialists and theorists in France, and which is reflected in the very tenor of their communication style[1]. Add to this the fact that business executives in France read more novels than the national average (44% as compared with 31%)[2] and that *culture générale* as a mode of continuous training increasingly seeks to incorporate a literary element, and one begins to feel that any serious-minded student likely to do business - and by implication socially interact - in France, should have some opportunity of exposure to literature. The more relevant it is in the initial stages - that is, the more students are able to relate it to the central orientation of their studies - the more receptive they are likely to be. The value of an integrative approach, particularly on a modular degree, where the discrete elements can so easily add up to something less than a coherent whole, hardly needs emphasizing.

It has to be admitted that one of the difficulties in developing this module was to identify texts which explored characters and relationships in the specific context of a "modern" working environment or organisation, and which had as a key focus the human factor in the workplace. A year's long search in France failed to come up with anything approaching David Lodge's *Nice Work*. With the exception of a sociological-based text - *Travailler deux heures par jour* (Adret) - the title of which was sufficient to allure one, and a slight, racy, feminist novel by a virtually unknown author, Dorothée Letessier - *Le Voyage à Paimpol* - which struck echoes of Loti, it was necessary to make a virtue of necessity and fall back on texts used in earlier years for a more general literature and society course, namely, *325 000 francs* (Roger Vailland), *Les Belles Images* (Simone de Beauvoir) and *Elise, ou la vraie vie* (Claire Etcherelli)[3]. It was surprising, however, when viewed from the particular angle described below, how much these texts yielded. In retrospect, I regretted not having substituted *Bernard Quesnay* (André Maurois) for one of them, so as to include a more sustained exploration of the theme of management in a bourgeois industrial context, and viewed from the perspective of management itself. However dated in certain of its aspects this novel might be, the type of human problems and dilemmas it explores as confronting managers in their day-to-day existence, as well as its analysis of the fatal lure of business for one who is born with business in his blood, have an enduring interest and significance.

The integrative framework

From an introductory reflection on different connotations of the word *travail*, to which each student contributed - (responses were wide-ranging, but revealed an interesting preponderance of what may be termed personal over material or financial goals, for example, *trouver de la satisfaction, gagner du respect, s'exprimer, affirmer sa personnalité, rencontrer des gens de tous genres* [sic]) - there followed a brief historical survey of the development of work organisations, with particular reference to Taylorism and its legacy. The laying of a theoretical framework for discussion of the individual case-studies to follow was completed by a student-centred analysis, facilitated by work-sheets, of a variety of source materials in French, which focused on the concept of the modern work organisation. These included a thought-provoking article from *L'Express* on the "new-style firm", extracts from Georges Archier's and Hervé Sérieyx's much acclaimed book, *L'Entreprise du 3e Type*, and an up-to-date video (obtained from the Centre Audio-Visuel de l'Entreprise) on participative management - *La Dynamisation Sociale dans l'Entreprise*. Thus were established certain basic themes and concepts - and the language with which to deal with them - as a framework of reference for the concrete individual cases subsequently explored, namely

le divorce et la réconciliation entre les notions de homme-travail
les ressources humaines comme source de richesse
la mobilisation créative et la valorisation de l'individu
la formation

le travail d'équipe et la communication
les responsabilités humaines des dirigeants
la politique sociale de l'entreprise.

As regards the order of approach for the texts selected, it was decided, for a variety of reasons, to start with the authentic situations presented in *Travailler deux heures par jour*. These take the form of a number of *témoignages* or interviews with a variety of workers - interestingly used by Zeldin in his book, *The French*, as indicative of modern day workers' attitudes in France - to support the general thesis that a more just, egalitarian system could be developed which would reduce the meaningless drudgery of all and at the same time lessen the cleavage of class. The reality of work for all of the individuals interviewed - these included a textile worker, a secretary in a research laboratory, a post-office worker and a docker - was a stark contradiction of the principles established in the opening lectures. The early inclusion of this text thus gave students a more rounded and critical view of what may be termed the working machine, and an appreciation in particular of the fundamental problem of class attitudes and their impact on the workplace and the process of production. From a more practical point of view the interviews, which were succinct and expressed the concrete experiences and moral attitudes of the individuals concerned in a terse, down-to-earth, often emotive language which posed few difficulties of comprehension, provided an ideal opportunity for student presentations, these being part of the assessment package for the module. By incorporating these at an early stage, it was hoped to encourage a good level of student participation and involvement, in preparation for the literary based part of the module to follow, and also to develop confidence in oral expression and debating techniques. In terms of their content, moreover, these short factual cases highlighted a number of social, psychological and ethical questions of central relevance to the novels subsequently explored and thus served as a useful transition to them, whilst the more general emphasis on such themes as consumerism, productivism, and waste fixed the debate firmly in the present and a socio-economic environment to which the students could relate.

Conveniently the number of cases included in the text, with the addition of two related topics of core significance, meant that students were able to work in pairs. They were each given a standard set of questions to explore, either as a framework or as a starting-point for their presentation. These focused on factors which contributed to satisfaction or dissatisfaction in the workplace, on symptoms of the latter, and solutions which might be envisaged. As well as analysing the text for the appropriate information, they were encouraged to present their own ideas and to pose questions which broadened up the discussion and involved the class as a whole.

In most cases students responded well to the challenge, and the sort of questions they asked extended the discussion beyond the concrete and particular to more abstract and speculative issues. Thus, for example, the question with which one group concluded, "*le travail est-il pour nous ou contre nous?*", led into an interesting analysis of the notions of *nécessité*, *liberté*, and *fatalité*. The example of another worker, who had rebelled against what seemed to be a typical management disregard in France for the most basic personality and communication needs of its workers and found refuge in the more human values of the Maghreb, led a student to question whether the word "civilisation" was compatible with industrialisation and thus to an attempt to define the notion. A more general point to emerge from most of the cases analysed was a typically French preoccupation with *le sens*, even the lowest placed worker seeking a justification for his situation, which reflected a certain abstract awareness of himself and his condition. To what extent this left its mark on the students it would be difficult to say. There was, however, a good level of involvement and exchange of ideas in this part of the module. This, together with progress in the more material aspects of presentation technique, such as the production and effective use of transparencies, coordination and team work, and the development of general oral confidence, made this a highly rewarding part of the course.

Fictional cases

As has been indicated, one of the problems, as regards the fictional cases subsequently explored, was a certain repetitiveness of theme and working situation. With the exception of *Les Belles Images* (though even here the themes were introduced obliquely) the emphasis was very much on the degrading and alienating nature of production line work, on capitalist exploitation and on the cleavage of class. In spite of this there was sufficient variety of character and social context, as well as range of treatment, to focus in each novel on a particular theme, which was then developed through a system of cross-reference to principles and ideas already established, in order to draw out its more general significance to the contemporary world. An attempt moreover was made, as we progressed through the cases, gradually to interrelate these discrete elements or themes into a more total construct or view, so that they provided a coherent learning experience.

Thus in *325 000 francs*, the emphasis was on the theme of enterprise. The potentially positive aspects of enterprise, both individual and social, as they are alluded to in the novel - dominance of one's situation, attachment to the principles of liberty and independence, the maximization of energy and initiative, its role in relation to job creation, to the material and social (and by implication educational) improvement of the workers, and to economic progress generally - were contrasted with its negative aspects as they are actually demonstrated (though here the ideological stance of the author was underlined) - greed, egoism, exploitation of one's fellows, the pursuit of status as an end in itself. The failure to harmonize the talents and creative energies of the individual with the needs of the larger community, resulting in a cleavage which ultimately leads to tragedy, was related above all to a lack of social consciousness, seen in this novel as the principal shortcoming of the "managing" class.

This was the theme subsequently explored in *Les Belles Images*. There were scores of examples provided by the bourgeois technocrats, who constitute the principal "worker-class" explored in this novel, of their ignorance of, if not contempt for, the lives of those who are the supposed beneficiaries of the economic revolution they themselves are driving. Perhaps the most striking was the main protagonist's utter indifference to the "image" of the young girls working in the canning factory, condemned to the same relentless gesture for every minute of their working day, an image which so disturbs her daughter and her schoolfriend. It was the social conscience of these two youngsters, revealed in particular in their preoccupation with the working lives of adults and their own career aspirations, which became the focus of discussion in this novel. As the next generation of workers their career choices (agriculture in the case of the one and medicine of the other), determined by their sense of social responsibility and the desire to fight against poverty, suffering and the exploitation of the poor by the rich -an awareness stimulated above all by the media - were set against those of their parents and the values underlying them, in particular the obsession with wealth, status and class. This focusing on the theme of career and vocation allowed one to home in again on the central character and her enviable -judged by appearances - job in advertising, which satisfied so many of the criteria discussed in the opening lecture: her job is intellectually and imaginatively stimulating, gives her a wide range of contacts, economic freedom and social status. The interest of her situation, however, was seen to lie in the gradual penetration of appearances to expose the myth of wealth and glamour and consumerism, seen here however from a quite different perspective from that in the previous novel. She too was seen to have been alienated, dehumanized by her working situation, not by the stultifying repetition of the same endlessly repeated gestures, but by her constant exposure to images, self-created, upon which her working life gravitates. Her obsession with objects and their appearances, as they appeal to the consumer, has the effect, psychologically, of limiting her to a world of surfaces and artificiality, which gradually erodes her sense of inner reality and the capacity to feel or to respond as a human being. The comment by one of the characters that not only is there "le malheur des pauvres... Il y a aussi celui des riches" (p.149) was interpreted in particular, in the context of our discussions, in the sense of the quality of life of the characters as affected by their working situation, and comparisons were made between the two novels from this point of view. The question was again raised as to whether "life" and "work" were to be viewed as separate or interdependent notions. This subsequently formed the basis of the essay which students wrote, as the second part of their assessment, the essence of which they derived from a more personal analysis of the texts studied.

A further important dimension of the "work" theme in *Les Belles Images* is that of the working mother, seeking to reconcile the demands made on her by her career, and those imposed upon her by her family situation. This theme provided an effective link with the third novel studied, *Le Voyage à Paimpol*, which focuses on a similar problem, but as experienced by a woman from the working class. As regards the working situation presented - here an OS doing a production line job - but in particular the social attitudes displayed by her towards her fellow-workers, this novel could not be further removed from the previous one. The central character's social conscience, her union involvement and militancy, her longing for a "profession", because it will provide her with a salary which will allow her to give to third-world charities and devote her leisure to social and educational causes, form a striking contrast with the self-preoccupation and social indifference of the previous protagonist. Her reflections on her role and activities as a *déléguée du personnel* and her evocation of typical scenes with management to negotiate better deals on wages, working conditions, health and safety, and training provide, in addition, a vivid and realistic picture of the workings of the *comité d'entreprise*, but more especially, perhaps, a cynical exposure of the myth of democracy and participation, as these operate in certain organisations, and of the abuse of hierarchy and power. The principles of enlightened management introduced earlier through the video, in particular the notions of "valorisation" and "self-realisation", were seen to be contradicted by every aspect of her working situation which, as she herself wryly comments, gave her not "de la valeur, mais des rides" and "des heures d'absence d'[elle]-même". (p.139)

It was precisely this "absence" from herself which she was seen to have in common with the chief protagonist of the previous novel, the overriding effect of work for both of them being to set them on a quest for existential meaning. If the root obstacles to life within their working situation are in each case different, in the latter case "une vie programmée" and the sacrificing of the individual "sur l'autel de la production", (p.141) the symptoms are more or less identical. Her flight to Paimpol, which is a temporary reprieve from the soul-destroying routine, stress and subjection of work, both in the factory and family, is conveyed essentially, like the previous protagonist's escape to Greece, as an attempt to recover a true sense of identity.

It was the theme of work as related to the quest for meaning and identity, which was highlighted in the final novel studied, *Elise ou la vraie vie*. Whilst the material aspects of the heroine's working condition were more or less identical with those described in *Le Voyage à Paimpol*, interestingly their effect on her character and development were seen to be quite different. The very word "development" is significant here. Whilst the idea of reality or *la vraie vie* was particularly associated in the heroine's mind, in the earlier part of the novel, with introspection and a certain form of timeless isolation from the world, gradually it was seen to be identified with her harrowing experience at the assembly line itself. It is there, amidst the deafening roar of machinery and the stench of oil, and subjected to every sort of indignity, that she comes to acquire a fuller sense of existence. This was explained by reference to her discovery of, and sense of insertion in, other lives or destinies, subjected to time or history.

It was these two associated themes which provided the focus for discussion. The novel allowed first of all an elaboration of the idea put forward by one of the students in the opening lecture, that a key value of work was to draw one from the confines of a particular milieu or class to discover different attitudes, values and life-styles. The chief character's experience of working alongside immigrants and other deprived individuals was seen to be a deeply humanizing experience and of crucial importance to her personal development or education. It was this theme of personal development which led to a different interpretation of the idea of time, as affecting the workers and their perception of life, from that which had been developed in *325 000 francs*. There, work was seen to be morally destructive essentially because the individual had no relation to time. The same gestures endlessly repeated - "et rien d'autre jusqu'à la mort" (p.52) - meant that the individual, like a "thing", was bounded by the present, without a future and without a past. Here, on the contrary, work becomes part of the "adventure" (with all the temporal connotations this word implies) of living. A further and related factor, which students undoubtedly came to appreciate in relation to the theme of immigrant labour, was the educative importance of history in enabling one to act in the workplace in full social consciousness of one's situation.

There was thus a great deal of overlap between the novels. Whilst the focus of the analysis remained the individual in relation to the working environment, it was interesting to note how often one was brought back to traditional literary themes such as time, freedom, fatality, each of the novels raising the question of the extent to which the individual in the workplace is able to control - or as a modern human resource text in French might put it - to be an "actor" in his own destiny. The essay already referred to provided students with a more personal opportunity to pull the various themes together and, at the same time - since it was written in French - to measure their own linguistic gains.

Evaluation

A questionnaire survey carried out at the end of the course allowed an evaluation of it from the students' point of view. The questionnaire was completed in class time, with no prior warning being given, and in the interests of truth and spontaneity they were asked not to sign it. For the most part, there was a close correlation between student evaluation of the various aspects of the course and my own.

Seen from my point of view, the most obvious and measurable gains were in the field of language acquisition - a prime consideration, given the applied nature of the course. The focusing on certain themes which recurred from novel to novel, and by reference to key human resource issues which had been established in the opening lectures, meant that by the end of the course students were handling naturally and spontaneously such linguistic items as *le facteur humain, se réaliser, valoriser l'individu, les attentes de l'individu, l'ouvrier robot, la parcellisation, le gaspillage*. Students themselves were very positive about the linguistic benefits they had derived from the module. They felt it had "definitely improved [their] language skills", "it [had] developed reading skills" and "listening comprehension [had] greatly improved"; "it gave a lot of opportunity for speaking", and "an increased and enriching vocabulary"... "a wider range of vocabulary than before - description, narration, speech"; "the same vocabulary appeared again and again, and it was an enjoyable way of learning it"; "it gave confidence in expressing one's views".

Perhaps the major benefit of the course, however, from the students' point of view, was its contribution to their intellectual and personal development. They expressed above all their appreciation of the "ideas" content of the course, which undoubtedly explained the good level of participation and involvement; if they communicated well, this was because they felt they had something to communicate about. They commented, for example, that they had been "made to think deeply about issues not usually discussed in other modules"... "about life issues"; "the various aspects of "working" were developed beyond the normal range of discussion". There were interesting personal revelations, one student commenting that the course had made her "consider [her] mercenary attitude towards work and [her] own egoistic desire to succeed, though not at the expense of others".

One may sum up the positive aspects of the course, therefore, by saying that students had developed considerably their communicative potential. They had extended significantly their lexical range, developed their comprehension and reading skills, and their ability to handle abstract ideas both in speech and in writing. They were able to use French as native speakers of French, to deal with fundamental issues relating to their professional or working lives. Literature had thus served as a facilitator of authentic and natural expression. To this extent its role was amply justified, whatever nagging doubts occasionally assailed me when the literary purist took over, and I sought to focus, for example, on questions of style and structure, interludes which were characterized by virtual silence. The intention had not been to teach literature "for itself" (if such an approach is in any case valid, except for a small minority of students with a true literary bent). On this issue it may be emphasised that both reactions during the course and feedback afterwards were at variance with C Evans' findings in his survey, "Modern Linguists and the Study of Literature". The approach to literature adopted had presented no problem of "negotiation across a generation gap", revealing students who were "cautious, compliant, and nervous of going too deeply into things". They were not "being asked to read and demonstrate reading at a level which [was] beyond them", but were learning the art of reading naturally, to achieve "growth and self-discovery"[4]. Moreover they seemed actively to be enjoying the experience, and to be developing a more open mind to reading. Contrary to my expectations, they had not found the books repetitive, but had appreciated the individual treatment by authors of similar themes, even though - and understandably - they felt that "a book from the eighties would have been an interesting addition". It was noticeable that when cross-reference was made to other writers, for example Flaubert - interestingly *bovarysme* was a theme which continually intruded - students took note, as though the will and intention were there to read further. Perhaps the most interesting response, which came out under "Any other comments" - and this surely points to the value of an integrative approach - was that they had enjoyed expressing ideas about themselves and about life, through having a new language at their disposal. Some of the students, at least, had experienced something approaching the stimulus of creative expression. It was the odd moments when the spark was discharged which were the most rewarding, from a teaching point of view.

It may be suggested in conclusion, therefore, that the particular advantages of this approach were to remove not only the barrier - or "false antonym", as J. Roach refers to it[5] - between language and literature, but also between business studies and literature. Linguistic and literary gains had been subsumed under what may be termed transferable personal gains which, whilst relevant to the students' education as a whole, had in certain of their applications a particular relevance to business. Correspondingly with the principles of the Enterprise and Capability movements, students had developed greater personal effectiveness. One is, of course, on dangerous territory, academically, here and it would be easy to make wild, undemonstrable claims. The students' own comments nevertheless suggest that they felt themselves more mature individuals, better able to communicate about issues of importance, concerning in particular their working lives. They had surely developed in particular their "people skills" (as the "capability" experts refer to it!) The response to a question in the evaluation survey on the students' comparative experience of the French, as set against the business "People in Organisations" module, pointed to their appreciation of an extra dimension in the literature-based approach, which may perhaps best be summed up as an approximation to real-life experience. The course "showed what life is like for people, rather than concentrating on theory". Should one infer from this that the issue of theory and practice is just as relevant to undergraduate business teaching as it is central to the current debate on the MBA, and that practice does not necessarily mean physical presence in a firm? One should beware of carrying the logic of the argument too far, but perhaps the old humanist adages on the virtue of literature to enlarge human sympathies and understanding and to give a deeper perception of the interrelatedness of life are not without their relevance to it. A fascinating consideration here is that it is just such principles of the imagination and understanding and the larger life-view which, as indicated above, make the uniqueness of certain specialist French texts on human resource management. The experiment had provided a basis for collaboration between linguists and business specialists in the interests of a holistic approach to learning which would be of benefit not only to students but also to staff[6].

To what extent is the approach outlined relevant to other vocationally or professionally oriented degree courses? Clearly approaches in one institution (or faculty) are not automatically transferable to another, since they so often depend for their effectiveness on the interests and predispositions of individuals. Given however the linguistic as well as personal benefits students appeared to have derived from the approach outlined, I would suggest there is a strong argument for offering a similar type of applied literature module on other combined degrees, such as French with architecture or French with environmental, hospitality or tourism management. In none of these areas would literary cases with a professional content be difficult to find. Could any manual on architecture, for example, give such an intimate feeling for the vernacular architecture of Burgundy or its special tourist or environmental appeal, whilst at the same time giving such a rich linguistic feast, as Henri Vincenot's *Le Pape des escargots?* Clearly mathematics and science-based subjects pose more of a problem. I incline more and more to the view, however, that a literary component has a place on such courses. This is not only for the linguistic benefits it offers, but also in order to put the language study in its proper human and cultural perspective. As J. Roach so rightly reminds us, "French literature is an essential part of French civilisation, it is essential for the French, to their language and for our understanding of both"[7].

Notes

1. See, for example, Archier, G., and Sérieyx, H. (1984) *L'Entreprise du 3e type,* Seuil.

2. Dollé, C,. and Santini, S. (5-18 decembre 1991) "Industries culturelles: le filon cadres", *L'Expansion,* p.58.

3. Adret, (1977) *Travailler deux heures par jour,* Seuil (Points Actuels).
Dorothée Letessier, (1980) *Le Voyage à Paimpol,* Seuil.
Roger Vailland, (1975) *325 000 francs,* English Universities Press.
Simone de Beauvoir, (1980) *Les Belles Images,* Heinemann Educational Books.
Claire Etcherelli, (1985) *Elise ou la vraie vie,* Methuen Twentieth Century Texts.

4. Evans, C. (1986) "Modern Linguists and the Study of Literature",
Communicative Approaches in French in Higher Education, AFLS Occasional Papers 1, pp.63-6.

5. Roach, J. (1988) "Civilisation now", *AFLS Newsletter 19,* p.17.

6. A further example at Leeds of the development of this type of collaboration in the interests of synergy is in the field of Public Relations and European Marketing and Languages. See Adams, Parry, Sheard and Webb, " The Integration of Languages and Business on a business modular programme", paper presented at Higher Education for Capability Conference, October 1992 (proceedings to be published by Kogan Page, December 1992).

7. *op. cit.*, p. 17.

Integration horizontale
ou
Profession : enseignant.

Savoir être généraliste

Geneviève Parkes, University of Portsmouth

Pour les régimes, on recommande déjà la méthode globale. Inutile, n'est-ce pas, d'acheter du pain en tranches à basses calories si c'est pour le recouvrir de beurre et d'une généreuse couche de confiture. Les nouveaux outils d'enseignement de la langue ont d'immenses mérites, qu'il s'agisse de programmes d'ordinateurs à usage individuel, de vidéo interactive, de musique de fond relaxante, mais trop souvent, la confiance que l'on a en eux tient plutôt d'un optimisme déplacé que de lucides références à la réalité. Les anglophones en particulier, de nature peu enclins à s'encombrer d'autres langues puisque la leur est si utile et si valorisée, recherchent moins la véritable compétence qu'une rentabilité utopique - comparez à ce propos les méthodes d'apprentissage de prédilection et leurs messages publicitaires en Grande-Bretagne et en France. «Parlez anglais comme les Anglais» (journaux, revues hebdomadaires pour les contacts soutenus et multiples), mais "Learn French in Three Weeks" (méthodes "accélérées" ou "magiques").

Naturellement, vous connaissez autant de clients satisfaits dans l'un et l'autre cas que de ménagères souriantes sorties deux fois plus vite de leur cuisine après avoir acheté le produit miracle qui fait «tout briller sans frotter».

A force de rechercher les techniques les plus appropriées et les plus performantes, de mesurer l'impact de leur efficacité par des instruments de mesure toujours plus précis, l'on risque d'oublier le contexte de l'apprentissage.

Il s'agit, comme lorsque l'on gère une entreprise, de transformer les conditions extérieures, qui peuvent être considérées comme autant de freins, de difficultés, et au mieux comme des éléments neutres à oublier, en atouts à exploiter dans la mesure du possible: si l'on ne dispose pas du temps que l'on souhaiterait utile pour enseigner une langue étrangère, que par ailleurs l'on soit pris par des cours de civilisation, d'histoire, d'économie, de littérature etc. avec les mêmes élèves, l'une des mesures à prendre au plus tôt est de décompartimenter. Difficile, certes, dans le contexte actuel de la situation qui affecte l'enseignement des langues dans le supérieur en Grande-Bretagne : les postes de haut niveau en didactique d'enseignement des langues étrangères sembleraient avoir disparu. Sont recherchés des spécialistes en histoire, gestion, sociologie etc. en mesure - accessoirement - de parler et d'enseigner la langue du pays de leur spécialité. L'enseignement des langues risque d'être de plus en plus cantonné dans une position annexe : comme tous les étudiants, quelle que soit la nature de leurs études, sont considérés maintenant comme des consommateurs potentiels (parler une langue étrangère doit leur être utile de nos jours, n'est-ce pas?, tout comme le maniement des ordinateurs et la pratique d'un sport), les *Language Centres* et les programmes globaux d'enseignement des langues étrangères (*IWLP*) se développent. Il leur faut un directeur - expérience en gestion et en marketing souhaitée - et des exécutants, trop souvent recrutés - économie oblige - comme vacataires, lumpenprolétariat de CDD[1], de lectrices, d'enseignants diplômés, chômeurs à temps partiel, payés à la tâche. Les postes des collègues linguistes ayant atteint l'âge de la retraite se transforment, parfois progressivement et discrètement, parfois d'un coup, sans autre forme de procès, en nouveaux contrats pour civilisationnistes, juristes, historiens, etc., pour peu qu'ils sachent s'exprimer en langue étrangère.

Le fait d'enseigner les langues étrangères au niveau Bac + 3 ou 4 se heurte souvent à des problèmes de motivation:

> Grâce à l'enthousiasme et au travail du linguiste débutant, les progrès sont souvent visibles et satisfaisants. La langue, de cible devient outil, et renforce la connaissance. C'est le cercle vertueux.

> Malheureusement, l'énergie s'essouffle. Au niveau universitaire, de par la nature-même des choses, l'étudiant s'enrichit moins au bout d'une heure de cours de langue que lors de ses premières armes. En fin de

parcours, disons au niveau de la licence, l'année à l'étranger est venue ajouter une impression (fallacieuse, cela va sans dire) de compétence - lorsqu'on sait dire «tous les jours, je suis allée bouffer avec deux mecs au RU mais la nourriture était dégueulasse», on parle français, n'est-ce pas?

Le phénomène d'absentéisme en cours de langue est hélas connu et il incombe aux enseignants de trouver des moyens non-punitifs d'y remédier; en gros, il s'agit de démontrer que ce que l'on apprend en cours est utile. C'est aussi dans ce but que se développent les cours de Français des Affaires, Français pour Ingénieurs etc., louables projets mais qui ne doivent pas faire oublier la posologie ou les modes d'administration.

Les cursus recommandent religieusement la consultation et la coordination entre enseignants: que les cours de langue s'inspirent des programmes : textes tirés de l'oeuvre étudiée en littérature, discussions sur les thèmes de civilisation, rédactions en français sur l'Affaire Dreyfus étudiée en histoire; on prône l'approche interdisciplinaire, l'intégration des différents éléments enseignés dans un cursus, à un niveau donné de progression, que l'on pourrait appeler intégration horizontale.

Cette coordination, telle qu'elle est recommandée, est souvent plus facilement imprimée sur les programmes distribués en début d'année universitaire que dans la réalité quotidienne.

Pour qu'elle soit efficace, il faudrait que soient réunis de façon constante plusieurs paramètres:

- une gestion des cursus centralisée doublée des moyens de communication appropriés (y compris proximité géographique et lieu de rencontre accueillant pour les enseignants),

- une équipe unie, motivée, plus préoccupée du bien public que de la réussite professionnelle individuelle de ses membres,

- des équipements de fonctionnement (bibliothèque y compris bibliothèque sonore, matériel informatique et vidéo, secrétariat, support technique, photocopieuses etc.) infaillibles.

L'intégration horizontale: interdisciplinarité et interaction de la langue et des matières d'application - mais dans les deux sens (la langue ne servant pas uniquement d'outil) représente cependant l'une des solutions aux problèmes de motivation. Les difficultés pratiques de coordination (exacerbées par les rétrécissements de budget, l'augmentation du nombre des étudiants, et l'érosion des conditions de travail des enseignants) ne doivent pas y constituer un obstacle. Il existe une approche plus simple... Les restrictions budgétaires des années 80 m'ont donné l'occasion de pratiquer cette intégration globale horizontale (nécessité mère de l'invention!). La désaffection pour les enseignements "classiques" (langue et littérature) s'accompagnant à la fois de diversification des intérêts vers l'économie, le marketing, la gestion en particulier, et de licenciements de collègues (s'effectuant souvent de façon inversement proportionnelle aux besoins en présence), il était inévitable que ce soient précisément les 'littéraires' qui se recyclent en gestion et en marketing.

Grâce à l'aide à la formation des formateurs, j'ai ainsi pu transformer un vâgue intérêt en un outil d'enseignement. Nous venions de perdre, pour raisons de changement de carrière, notre collègue francophone spécialiste en économie et sciences politiques qui assurait les travaux dirigés de marketing en langue française (L'option d'initiation au marketing est proposée aux étudiants en licence de français). L'utilisation d'un vacataire aurait sans doute fait perdre 'l'esprit de l'option' (tout enseignant se chargeant par exemple des cours d'économie théorique et appliquée pour les étudiants de première et de deuxième années et de marketing pour l'année de licence contribue à la notion d'intégration verticale, de cohérence du diplôme), et l'utilisation d'un consultant spécialiste aurait peut-être fait perdre l'utilisation de la langue-cible.

Après obtention de certificats de marketing (préparation par correspondance) proposés par l'*Open Business School*, j'ai pu reprendre cette responsabilité annexe (les cours magistraux ainsi qu'une partie des TD étant assurés - en anglais - par un spécialiste "prêté" par le département d'économie/ gestion/ marketing).

Les étudiants de Portsmouth s'inscrivant de plus en plus nombreux en option marketing, je me suis soudain retrouvée institutrice (spécialiste en tout genre) avec nos candidats en année de licence; ils ne pouvaient m'échapper: grammaire, labo, France Contemporaine, et désormais marketing! Pour la dimension "française" en marketing, non seulement nous nous penchons sur des études de cas basées sur la France (ou d'autres pays francophones), mais dans la mesure du possible, pour chaque étudiant anglophone, est inscrit un étudiant francophone, aimablement mis à ma disposition par notre Diploma in English Studies - il s'agit d'étudiants d'échange (étudiants Erasmus ou inscrits à titre individuel) venant passer deux trimestres ou une année universitaire à Portsmouth; ce diplôme d'anglais langue étrangère est pour la plupart d'entre eux comptabilisé comme équivalence partielle ou totale de leurs diplômes en cours dans leurs universités d'origine. Ces étudiants étrangers peuvent choisir Marketing comme option, les cours magistraux se déroulant en anglais). Les exposés de TD sont présentés par deux étudiants, un francophone et un anglophone, nous pouvons donc être sûrs qu'au moins l'un des deux aura fait l'effort de travailler dans sa langue cible!

Donc le français sert à enseigner le marketing, mais le marketing devient aussi outil de l'enseignement de la langue : en effet, au niveau initiation (et c'est bien de cela qu'il s'agit pour nos étudiants en langues), le marketing est une matière particulièrement adaptée à l'interaction langue/matière d'application: de la même manière que M. Jourdain découvrait avec ravissement qu'il savait parler en prose, les étudiants se voient soudain pratiquants de marketing à leur insu - il suffit d'être consommateur, d'effectuer des choix de consommation, de connaître ou de reconnaître des produits ou des services. Dans cette optique pédagogique, on pourrait comparer le marketing à la sociologie ou à la psychologie : sans se prétendre sociologue ou psychologue, toute personne sensée peut formuler certaines remarques, ne serait-ce que subjectives, appuyées sur des expériences de vie. Ces sciences reposent sur nombre de faits "quotidiens", beaucoup de leurs thèmes font l'objet de conversations ou de débats courants. Le marketing est lui aussi mise en ordre et en perspective d'hypothèses, basées sur des cas, reposant sur des statistiques et formulées sous forme de théories, qui sont suivies avec enthousiasme par certains praticiens, réfutées par d'autres, fluctuant selon les modes. Le marketing n'est ni vente, ni publicité, ce à quoi il est parfois réduit aux yeux des néophytes, bien que vente et publicité fassent partie des techniques de commercialisation appelées parfois "la mercatique" mais plus généralement "le marketing".

Il est question d'études de marché, de lancement de produits, d'études de portefeuilles de produits, de choix de circuits de distribution des biens et des services, de politiques de prix, et d'activités de promotion (VRP[2], promotion sur lieu de vente, publicité gratuite , démarches publicitaires etc.).

Ce rapide survol permet de voir à quel point ces sujets sont d'actualité et se prêtent au dialogue et aux échanges, donc à la pratique orale! pendant les TD.

De surcroît, la situation économique actuelle amène très souvent les étudiants de cet âge (Bac +3 ou + 4) à avoir eu des expériences de travail en entreprise, qu'ils peuvent exploiter lors des discussions et des analyses. Les étudiants sont ainsi à même a priori d'avoir des opinions, des expériences à exploiter; l'élément comparatif s'ajoute de soi par la présence du milieu hétérogène (il y a parfois aussi des étudiants d'autres nationalités, acceptés aux cours si leur niveau de français est assez élevé). La participation crée ainsi l'intérêt, qui assure à son tour une pratique suivie. La lectrice se présentant à son cours de conversation en proposant de parler de la pêche, de l'IVG ou de la pollution ne peut donc pas rivaliser...

Toutes ces raisons m'amènent donc à recommander tout particulièrement le marketing pour renforcer l'enseignement de la langue. Les travaux dirigés se déroulent en langue-cible, les étudiants de deux nationalités (ou plus) ont des idées et des opinions à échanger. Ils ont tous été consommateurs, ont tous effectué des choix d'achat, ont vu ou entendu des messages publicitaires, et certains d'entre eux ont travaillé pour des bureaux d'études de marché, ont vendu, géré, représenté, etc.

Il conviendrait de consulter d'autres enseignants "multicartes" et de se renseigner sur leurs expériences. Nul n'est à l'abri d'enthousiasme tendancieux...

En fait, il s'agit aussi et surtout de tirer parti d'une ubiquité que l'on pourrait qualifier d'intempestive. Lorsque la même personne assure les cours d'expression écrite, de France Contemporaine, etc., il n'y a pas besoin de note de service pour rappeler les thèmes traités ou enjoindre la coordination. Je conseille la pratique d'une propagande linguistique éhontée à ceux qui se trouveraient dans une situation similaire: rien de tel pour réveiller un auditoire affichant quelque propensité à l'indolence ou à la passivité en cours que de s'arrêter au milieu d'une phrase où l'on parle de politique sociale depuis 1981, et de souligner qu'il s'agit d'un exemple parfait de l'utilisation du subjonctif dans une proposition exprimant le doute, conformément à ce qui a été expliqué en cours de grammaire lundi dernier. Dans les exercices de style et de registre, on notera l'effet choc de la phrase-même prononcée quelques jours plus tôt en cours de littérature ou de civilisation, rappelant les faits mentionnés (ex. «vous ne vous seriez tout de même pas attendu à ce que Chirac se déclare favorable à ce genre de sanctions!» - utilisée en l'occurence pour la révision de la construction du verbe *s'attendre à*).

La répétition étant la base de la profession d'enseignant, toute crainte de trop se répéter s'avérera superflue. Comment croire en effet qu'en dépit des 10 heures passées en cours à expliquer les différences d'usage entre l'imparfait et le passé composé, la plupart des étudiants ne semblent pas pour autant parvenir à maitrîser ces subtilités?

La concentration, par exemple celle des cours intensifs, éveille l'esprit et le fixe sur les points importants, fait appel à des efforts de mémoire, se rapproche de l'immersion globale - qui n'a naturellement plus à faire ses preuves - mais fait perdre la répétition "hors programme", qui donne souvent une dimension de réalité: faire en classe des exercices sur les phrases complexes commençant par "si" ou "quand" revêt un caractère plus immédat lorsque, pendant les cours magistraux des jours qui suivent, l'on s'arrête après avoir prononcé «*Si* la théorie *avait été* prouvée *et qu'il soit* plus avantageux de...», et que l'on renvoie son auditoire à la leçon de grammaire appropriée.

A l'époque des premiers laboratoires de langue, le public croyait qu'il suffisait qu'on s'y enferme pendant 100 heures pour parler couramment une langue étrangère, ils tomberaient aujourd'hui presque en désuétude dans les universités qui forment les linguistes. Pour que les étudiants continuent à faire des progrès à un niveau élevé, la méthode aggrégative (expression écrite / expression orale / explication de texte / civilisation / etc.) ne suffit pas, même avec les meilleurs outils disponibles. Il faut attaquer à la fois l'inconscient *et* la prise de conscience. Trop répéter, trop prouver aux élèves qu'ils ont encore du chemin à parcourir, qu'on a rarement eu en main de groupe plus faible risque d'avoir des effets pervers et pour le moins décourageants.

Démontrer que ce que l'on fait le lundi après-midi est extrêmement utile pour le vendredi matin et ainsi de suite fait naître dans les esprits qui ont encore besoin d'en être persuadés, la persuasion que, d'une part, il y a toujours une application possible quel que soit l'objet d'étude, et de l'autre, qu'il est véritablement possible de s'améliorer en langue *après* un séjour même prolongé dans le pays.

Lorsqu'on est soi-même chargé de l'enseignement de plusieurs disciplines, il est aisé de faire resurgir de loin en loin des thèmes, des expressions, des idées "comme par hasard". L'étudiant convaincu qu'il n'a plus grand chose à apprendre, qu'il perd son temps aux cours, n'y apprendra presque rien (pour cause d'absence principalement). L'intégration horizontale - poussée jusqu'aux méthodes de propagande, risque de porter plus de fruits, y compris en ce qui concerne les clients récalcitrants.

Les nouvelles tendances de la restructuration des diplômes universitaires en Grande-Bretagne, rappelant le principe des *Unités de Valeur* risquent de générer de plus en plus de spécialisation. Difficile de prôner à la fois les avantages - pour l'étudiant - de ce système, et ceux de l'interdisciplinarité, menacée par l'arrivée de l'enseignement de masse et le recrutement systématique de spécialistes en domaines d'application. Non seulement certains de ces spécialistes (historiens, géographes, gestionnaires...) refusent d'enseigner la langue étrangère ou n'en sont pas capables, ou alors sont trop pris par leurs travaux de recherche et leurs publications, mais les enseignants de langue étrangère sont désormais trop souvent recrutés sur contrats peu motivants et n'ont ni le temps, ni la possibilité de vraiment rentabiliser au maximum leurs interventions. On a tendance à croire que l'amélioration des méthodes compensera ces choix discutables, mais n'oublions pas que l'apprentissage d'une langue étrangère comprend les trois angles du triangle (qui n'est pas nécessairement isocèle): l'apprenant, la langue, et les vecteurs de communication.

Notes

1. Contrat à Durée déterminée.

2. Voyageur Représentant Placier.